Shift!

How to Make Channel Shift Happen in Housing

ISBN 978-1-9164546-0-6

First published in 2018 by Prodo Digital.

Printed in Great Britain by Biddles Books Ltd.

Pippa Adams

Pippa is founder and CEO of Prodo, having started the digital agency in 1998.

She has been working with social housing clients for over 15 years, consulting with 40+ housing associations, delivering tangible benefits to the organisations and their customers. She also has a wealth of non-housing experience advising and delivering projects for numerous FTSE 250 companies; and as a result, she believes that the two share many of the same goals and enjoys taking the learnings from one sector and applying them to another to achieve their channel shift objectives. On a lighter note, she enjoys a good cup of

Rob Walker

Rob is Head of Product at Prodo and specialises in developing SaaS products for the social housing sector.

Rob is passionate about harnessing technology to transform and simplify complex services for the benefit of users and organisations alike. As a consultan in the housing space, he's worked closely with organisations to scope and deliver sector-leading, award-winning digital platforms. And having been employed in-house in both the public and private sectors, Rob is well versed in the intricacies of tackling large scale channel shift projects against a backdrop o

Contents

Preface

Only a decade ago, most mobile phones offered voice and text only, and the concept of the app was still new. By the end of the second decade of the twenty-first century, almost all mobile phones are smart, and booking transport, accommodation and accessing dozens of other services including banking, via such devices is an everyday occurrence for millions of people across the planet.

This gives an illustration of how rapidly technology has evolved and with it, our own habits and lifestyles too. It continues to evolve, along with many other technologies: the Internet of Things, autonomous vehicles and smart homes; Artificial Intelligence, augmented reality and virtual reality. Devices are not only getting smarter, they can talk to each other. Our collective digital activities can be tracked and monitored, yielding rich and detailed information on patterns of behaviour, that organisations can use to fine-tune their offerings by analysing what the resulting data is telling them. There are fridges that know when you've run out of milk and place an order; boilers that alert maintenance engineers when a part needs replacing, smart machines that can fix themselves and AI technologies that can predict behaviours and anticipate needs.

This is the fourth industrial revolution, a digitally interconnected world. Such rapid developments may provoke excitement, fear or bemused curiosity, but they cannot be ignored. They are changing the way in which all services are presented, and all businesses are run. This includes social housing – and the preferences of social housing tenants. Falling prices for smartphones mean that it is not only those owning their own homes who are plugged into social media and online banking.

Being digitally connected, with advanced mobile devices, is close to being universal.

Too often in business, technological innovation is understood in terms of the systems and the financial savings alone, and can provoke concerns over personal autonomy and privacy, and depersonalised customer service. In the social housing sector, the ultimate test of channel shift is: does it help the tenant enjoy an enhanced quality of life? This book describes how such technology can be intelligently and sensitively applied to this end. There are legitimate fears with the spread of mobile devices and digital information, especially as regards security – both personal security and data security – and personal privacy. In this, we can learn from other sectors and disciplines. Not only is technological innovation perfectly compatible with the abiding principles of social housing, but we will also show how it can help further the aims of providing secure, comfortable homes for some of the most vulnerable people in our society.

Developments in medical science are guided by the ancient principle 'First, do no harm.' Legislative change for the welfare of children honours the timeless principle 'The interests of the child come first.' In a similar way, technological innovation is best guided by the principle:

'Change must enhance quality of life.'

We are experienced at successfully and sensitively implementing automated systems in the housing sector. We know that some people love technology more than others, and we're okay with that. We have learned that it's best to work hard on the service, rather than proselytise about the wonders of all things digital. We don't spend much time 'selling' the benefits of technology. Rather, we dedicate that time to designing systems that make the experience so quick and stress-free that the customers become the advocates themselves.

In our work, we have become increasingly aware that the enormous potential of such shifts is not universally understood and that there seemed to be few publications specifically on this subject. We wanted to showcase the multiple benefits, reassure on some of legitimate fears, and create a practical handbook to help housing professionals implement the change effectively, drawing on best practice examples from within and outside housing. Above all, we have sought to emphasise that the benefits are social, as well as commercial and that, when sensitively implemented, they truly fulfil the humanitarian tradition of housing associations.

The knowledge base for this book extends well beyond our own experience. We carried out in-depth interviews with leading figures within the movement, many of whom are advanced in their implementation of channel shift, and conducted a questionnaire-based survey. While there may appear to be a certain irony in producing a printed book to extol the versatile features of digital connections, we fully recognise that traditional media perform a complementary role.

Channel Shift Survey 2018

87 UK housing organisations

205 respondents

C suite / Director	17.06%
Head of Service	10.59%
Manager	34.12%
Officer	38.24%

Another truth we have learned is that modernisation is continuous, to reflect the fact that technology is continually evolving, and that customers' needs may also alter over time. In addition, however, one-off project plans are sometimes necessary for introducing a particular technology. This combination, of continuous improvement and discrete projects, is an inevitable part of organisational adaptation in the fourth industrial revolution, and requires a sophisticated approach to management. It's necessary to involve the whole organisation, and understand its purpose. In practice, of course, while different specialisms need to be involved, there is a need to prevent project team membership becoming too wide and unmanageable.

Brian Halligan, CEO of Hubspot's comments echo this. He told us that **"from the very beginning of HubSpot, we decided not to go out and ask marketers what sort of features they wanted. That would have simply automated an outmoded way of doing marketing. Humans are constantly changing their expectations and behaviour with respect to how they find and buy products and services, and that's where we look to find the gaps in the current technology stack...Going forward, it means reversing the ratio of humans-to-automation in support of customer-facing functions – for example, moving much more to a try-before-buy process and to bot-supported conversations for repeatable and predictable inquiries."**

Discussion of robots and Artificial Intelligence is

often accompanied by a tacit belief that it's a zero-sum game; that the fullest implementation of channel shift will be greater efficiency, but a more impersonal service, and reduced opportunities for professional staff. Only the designers of the technology and the finance director will be pleased, so the theory goes.

This book exposes such a choice as false. It demonstrates instead that the smartest ways of automating services in social housing release caring workers from routine tasks, freeing them to do what they were trained for – helping to create strong and vibrant communities, supporting tenants whether they are professionals, families, elderly or otherwise vulnerable people. And channel shift can make essential services for tenants – paying rent, arranging repairs – easier, quicker and less stressful.

Why are we so confident that this happy blend of technological and social progress can be achieved? Because there is an established track record of successful implementations. The contributors to this book have decades of directly relevant experience of successful digital transformation projects in the corporate and non-profit sector between them. We can take the best lessons from the business world and apply them to social housing. This book is aimed at the people responsible for implementing change. You may have become aware that the means of collecting rent is antiquated, or that you have little data on tenants to guide service improvements, or that your call centre is overstretched, and dealing with matters that could be resolved in more convenient ways. You know things have to be improved. This book distils and presents advice from different successful adaptations.

Every healthy organisation's aim, whether in the for-profit or non-profit sector, is to enhance the quality of life of the customers it was set up to serve. And all successful implementation programs are focused around people. They begin and end with the people. The technology is the bit in the middle – the means to the end. This book is about a Shift; not a narrow shift from one technological channel to another, but a multidimensional and attitudinal shift towards enhanced connectivity and quality of life.

01
Evolution of the housing association:
From Victorian estates to the digital age

Samuel Lewis had humble beginnings. Born to a poor household in Birmingham in 1837, his father died when he was only 13.

He began work as a salesman, built up a jeweller's business, and later became a successful financier. He never forgot his origins, however, and had a strong social conscience. He and his wife Ada were particularly keen to improve the living conditions for those on the lowest income. His will left around £500,000 – almost £60million in today's money – specifically to social housing.

Accommodation for the working poor in the Victorian and Edwardian eras was often appalling, with no running water or toilets and overcrowded conditions. Starting with a new estate in Islington, North London in 1910, the Samuel Lewis Trust began developing blocks of apartments which, while modest by modern standards, were a vast improvement on the slums that came before. Samuel Lewis was not the only significant housing philanthropist of the time; another was George Peabody, who established the Peabody Trust. They were social pioneers; challenging the idea that those with humble beginnings should be condemned to live in squalid conditions. Slowly, the movement began to challenge and change such a neglectful attitude.

The housing association movement was born.

Through the Century

In the twentieth century, the housing sector was hugely influenced by the two world wars and the desire to demolish former slum areas, which were vulnerable to outbreaks of infectious diseases as well as being inadequate in terms of basic housing needs.

Such was the scale of the challenge that only the public sector could realistically take it on. In the decades immediately following the Second World War, the most significant providers were local authorities.

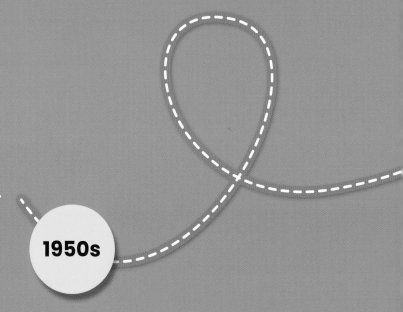

1950s

Bombing of cities led to an acute housing shortage and, by the mid-1950s, the government set itself the challenge of building 300,000 new homes a year.

It subsidised the construction of council homes, including a specific subsidy for blocks more than six storeys high. In every conurbation in the UK, tenement houses and rows of small terraced homes were replaced by high tower blocks, not all of which were successful in social terms.

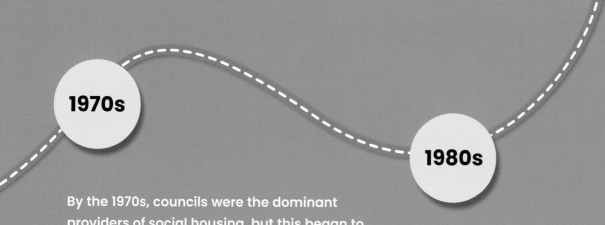

1970s

1980s

By the 1970s, councils were the dominant providers of social housing, but this began to change with major reforms brought in by the Thatcher government in the 1980s, which sharply reduced the incentives for local authorities to provide social housing directly.

First of all, the right to buy for council tenants, at a generous discount to market prices, proved extremely popular. This was especially the case with family homes, such that the publicly owned housing stock altered in its composition. The Government also prevented councils from using local taxes to subsidise council housing and directed grants for social housing to housing associations. In a parallel development in the post-war years, housing associations expanded their range of services from accommodation to the working poor, to include specialist housing for people with special needs such as mental health problems or addiction, and also for elderly people.

Since the 1980s, indirect consequences of the reforms, and of globalisation and a growing population, have meant that the role of housing associations is as important as ever.

High property prices, especially in the south-east of England, have led to a decline in home ownership. Globalisation has had a significant impact: in the private sector, it is common for entire blocks of new-build apartments to be purchased prior to completion by an international investment portfolio on a buy-to-let basis, not only in London but in cities such as Leeds and Manchester. This has meant a revival of the private rental sector, but often at rents that are beyond the reach of many households on lower incomes, especially in the Greater London area.

The Banking Crisis

Yet while the need for housing associations has been stronger than ever in recent years, the financial and political climate has been unfavourable in many ways. The banking crisis of 2008/09 made financing new housing projects difficult, as banks were forced to cut back sharply on fresh lending to repair balance sheets and meet stricter capital requirements.

Since then, rent controls have been tightened by the government, with a 1% cut to social market rents in 2016 helping affordability for tenants, but putting pressure on revenues for associations. Finally, reforms to the benefits system create a further squeeze. Universal Credit, being introduced at the time of writing, bundles several different benefits together, with the aim of increasing individual autonomy and encouraging a return to work. It means, however, that housing benefit is no longer paid directly to the landlord, which means social housing providers have to absorb the losses in cases where tenants have difficulty paying. As a result of all these changes, the credit ratings of some housing associations has been impacted.

In response to these pressures, there has been some consolidation, in the shape of mergers and acquisitions, among some of the approximately 1,700 housing associations across the UK. Scale can be a helpful response to the pressures to build more housing and attract finance, but of course, mergers pose formidable challenges in terms of integrating teams and harmonising IT platforms.

Another response from the sector to these changing circumstances has been an increasing focus on property development in the private sector, the profits from which help fund social housing. **Richard Eden** is Communications Manager at Southway, one such provider that has set up a commercial property wing; he acknowledges that this approach may have been seen as taboo by many in the sector, but he adds:

"We have to find ways to make money: what better way than in the field of expertise we are already in? We make them affordable, offer shared ownership; we're trying to fill that gap in between social housing and ownership."

21st Century

Some of the most significant changes of the twenty-first century are technological, rather than legislative or economic, and hold huge potential to absorb financial pressures while maintaining or enhancing services.

The digital age is not just about online shopping and holiday bookings. By opening up new ways of connecting people and delivering services, digital communication creates opportunities for social housing providers to improve services and make a positive impact on customers' lives whilst reducing running costs and streamlining their organisations.

Becoming a more customer-focused business does not mean losing the noble charitable ethos of the housing association; quite the contrary, it can mean enhancing quality of life for tenants. To grasp this point, it is helpful to challenge what is currently understood as a commercial approach, which can be understood in a narrow cynical way as placing profits ahead of people. Recent research by some business schools, however, shows that ethically run businesses can actually be more financially resilient over the longer term than those guided by quarterly earnings figures. The 'profit-at-all-costs' business model has hit crisis in recent years, with a succession of scandals: the Enron accounting affair, the sub-prime banking losses passed on to the taxpayer, interest-rate fixing by some banks, emissions test cheating by car manufacturers and many more. By contrast, many companies established on a more socially responsible ethos, such as family firms like Wates construction or WL Gore, continue to flourish and enjoy a strong reputation. This area is the subject of a growing movement among leading business thinkers, ethical entrepreneurs and management schools. It has led the World Economic Forum to refer to a New Paradigm, valuing social responsibility and long-term stewardship of companies, ahead of short-term profit maximisation and speculative trading of shares.[1] Even some corporations,

such as Unilever, have switched towards defining strategic objectives in social and environmental terms, rather than headline profits alone. A long-term research project on sustainable business by MIT Sloan and the Boston Consulting Group has found that, while such enlightened, responsible management of corporations is still a minority pursuit, the evidence that the approach yields strong business results, as well as better social outcomes, is compelling.[2]

This challenges a tacit notion that has been germane in social housing, that becoming more commercial means compromising a focus on social priorities and protecting the most vulnerable tenants. The old divide between social versus financial priorities is being challenged, as we learn new ways to help customers, employees and the business simultaneously.

[1] The New Paradigm: A Roadmap for an Implicit Corporate Governance Partnership Between Corporations and Investors to Achieve Sustainable Long-Term Investment and Growth, by Martin Lipton, World Economic Forum, September 2016

[2] Corporate Sustainability at a Crossroads, David Kiron et al, MITSloan Management Review Research Report, with the Boston Consulting Group, May 2017

Business Models

We define Business Model A as the traditional housing association and Business Model B as the conventional corporate approach.

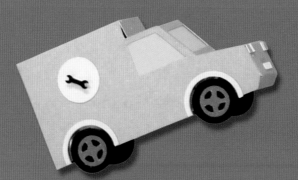

Business Model A
The 20th Century Housing Association

Key Features

- Strong social commitment, prioritising the needs of the vulnerable, sometimes ahead of business efficiency or maximising revenue.
- Departmental structure, featuring specialised roles.
- Tendency towards being suspicious of automation as diluting the 'human touch'.
- Heavily challenged by changes to Universal Credit and rent controls.

Business Model B
The 20th Century Corporation

Key features

- Focus on business efficiencies and revenue maximisation. Process-orientated.
- Views technology as a smart way of minimising headcount and maximising efficiencies.
- Guided by annual budgets and financial KPIs.
- Departmental structure.

With this framing, the choice facing those in the sector is unappealing, especially as revenue pressures would appear to compel leaders to choose Model B as the only viable option.

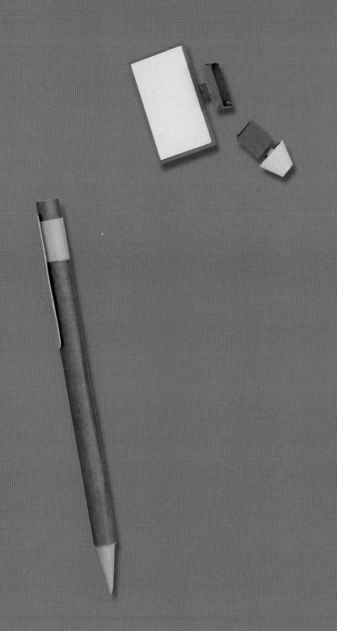

Interviewees for this book all note the increased commercialisation of the social housing sector in recent years. In part, this is owing to a squeeze on income through rent controls and changes in UK government policy such as the introduction of Universal Credit. Within this framing, a negative agenda could be assumed, with automation replacing human interaction to save costs, increasing social isolation against a backdrop of continued austerity for the sector and for tenants.

But a broader definition of 'commercialisation' to incorporate a concept of customer service, drawing on research on the business benefits of humane management, transforms the terms of reference of the debate and opens up a more optimistic agenda. Case studies from the private sector include socially responsible firms where the sense of purpose helps to encourage high levels of employee engagement. In turn, this helps companies become more agile and innovative, which is essential for responding to rapidly changing markets and technological change. Successful growing companies tend to feature high levels of cooperation and teamwork, and a more informal, less hierarchical culture than the conventional corporation.

If we introduce a third Business Model option, based on the experience of people interviewed for this book, and bolstered by research elsewhere in the global economy, a more palatable option emerges.

Business Model C
The 21st Century Agile Organisation

Key features
- Strong customer service ethos.
- Structured around teams and projects, not departments.
- Digitally savvy, but seeing communications technology as a means of enhancing quality of life as much as reducing unnecessary costs.
- Committed to continual innovation and improvement.

"

"I think, all the time I have worked in housing, there's a real sense of trying to ensure that tenants were treated as customers, but sometimes there's been a lack of understanding of what that meant."

Claire Bayliss
Consultant at 3C Consulting

Claire Bayliss, a consultant at 3C Consulting, says the biggest change in the housing sector in recent years is that: "We have woken up a bit. We're more commercial."

By the term "commercial" she means, primarily, a stronger sense of seeing things from a customer's point of view, rather than business process efficiencies. She recounts how a technical officer she had recruited in a former role spent six months at the supermarket firm Asda, went through their customer service training, and returned with far superior customer service ability. "His whole approach to interacting with customers was so different, that you suddenly realised we were behind. We had thought we had quite good customer service."

What had changed was "a combination of the language he used, the amount of listening he did. Although he didn't spend longer on calls, he gave the impression that he was giving a lot of time to the customer, because he was personally invested in getting it right for them. Not that we weren't, but we weren't able to get it across to the customer.

"I think, all the time I have worked in housing, there's a real sense of trying to ensure that tenants were treated as customers, but sometimes there's been a lack of understanding of what that meant."

Dan Moraga, Programme Manager for Digital Transformation at PA Housing, says his role involves transformation of the business, not just technology, with a view to being more agile and responsive to customers' needs. He says:

"We work with Prodo to take an agile approach. Very often we start with a clear idea of what we want and how to achieve it, but because a number of our solutions are complex, and because of customer feedback, we have to be quite flexible about how the projects work. It's an approach of continuous improvement, monitoring feedback from users. This has enabled us to zero in on the parts that are working really well, and also showed us what wasn't working – eg, no one's clicked; or they've clicked but we never saw a case resulting. It's a constant feedback loop going on. This is less effort than getting groups of customers to come in in office hours to discuss a certain path or process."

Boris Worrall, Chief Executive of Rooftop Housing Group, says that the sector is losing its "local authority" mindset and that, provided it retains its conscience, the trend is to be welcomed and encouraged.

"Society is changing around us. We're also gradually recruiting people from outside the sector; that has changed the [profile of] people who work in housing associations. There are two things to that: by orientation, we are good organisations, with 'nice' people, who tend to put people and society above profit. The drivers are good, ethical drivers. You don't want to lose that… [yet] there's a sense at the grassroots that face-to-face contact is a good thing; then a kind of implicit view that you cannot keep that with a digital service. But now others recognise that if you get digital right, you can offer a better customer service experience. That's starting to land."

Channel Shift Survey 2018

56% felt their customers were ready to self serve now

Another finding from the research for this book has been the extent to which tenants themselves are online, using mobile technology. The approach towards automating services until recently was framed in terms of the push or the 'nudge' required from business planners to encourage a channel switch from phone or face-to-face, but increasingly there is a 'pull' from customers wanting to connect via their mobile device to the housing provider in the same way that they do with their banks, supermarkets, retailers and more as we shall discuss further in later chapters.

Paul Taylor, Innovation Coach at Bromford Housing, has sought to incorporate lessons from outside the housing sector. "What struck me, and this relates to digital transformation, a lot of organisations who are good at innovation treat it with the same seriousness as their HR function, or strategic function."

Channel Shift Survey 2018

36% said their organisation didn't currently have a self service offering

He and his colleagues have set about encouraging such a culture at Bromford. He adds: "Innovation is a massively over-used word, usually misapplied. There are at least three crucial stages: the idea, the vision, which is the easy bit; the second part is doing something, moving on it; and the third is the added value, to internal processes or to the customer. A combination of those three things is innovation. Often people refer to it as the idea bit, rather than the execution of innovation; innovation is ultimately a process."

Such is the ubiquity of online connections and mobile technology that every company is a digital company nowadays. "We want booking a repair to be as easy as ordering a package on Amazon," as **Richard Eden**, Communications Manager at Southway Housing puts it. This blurs the distinction between housing and other sectors, and makes many roles interchangeable between sectors. Some of our interviewees working in housing associations have backgrounds in areas such as marketing, events management and so on in very different parts of the economy and their experience is directly relevant. **Paul Taylor** of Bromford adds:

"I think a change over the past few years is to learn that it's perfectly acceptable to have a different service offer. People have got bolder. RHP [Richmond Housing Partnership] has a very strong digital service, it differs from Bromford. It's now much more acceptable; we don't have to do things the same way. In the same way in banking, First Direct and Monzo bank are completely different offerings, and banking with them is different to opening an account with the Cooperative Bank, but they both carry out the same duty of looking after your money."

Several of our interviewees referred to the 'Smart City' of the future, with connected gadgets and integrated transport, which would result in the conventional housing association becoming very different as its services become integrated or in closer partnership with other services.

Robin Middleton, Head of Digital Marketing at Sovereign Housing, has a background in mobile communications and with an online bank. He and his team have built an IT infrastructure and an outlook more in line with global companies of a similar size than with a traditional housing association. He says:

"We're the same size as a FTSE 250 company. We are now moving in a similar way to a plc, to the companies I have worked with in the past. We may be a housing association, but we are in a global economy. We looked at what's best in a global context, not [IT] providers who are mainly in our sector. If the platform has more power, and ability in the future, it will prove to be a better investment. So a global platform gives us massive solutions and scope for future development."

Yet our interviewees are not losing sight of the social focus; all this modernisation and investment is a means to an end. Smart use of digital technology – as will be evidenced in later chapters – opens up new ways to connect people and build communities. Such reforms, when well implemented, can result in a virtuous circle of enhanced well-being and security for tenants, resulting in fewer social problems, failed tenancies and associated costs, enabling further investment in transformative technologies. Our research also found that digital forms of communication were enabling housing officers to hear more from people they had never heard from before because they shunned using the phone.

Building on these insights, digital connectivity gives business planners new ways to become more socially beneficial and more cost-effective simultaneously. Just as Samuel Lewis believed that the modern building standards of his day should be made available to those on modest incomes, digital pioneers in housing associations are ensuring that modern communications technology enhances quality of life for their tenants.

02
The future is now:
What services can look like

Signing up and moving in

Millions of applicants for residents of social housing in the UK still have to fill in lengthy paper forms when signing up for their tenancy.

When the boiler isn't working, tenants have to telephone a call centre, during opening hours, to arrange a repair, and wait in all day on the assigned date for the maintenance engineer to fix it. The housing association's staff's experience can be similarly time-consuming. A housing officer has to manually input all the information from an application form into a housing management system. In the case of a tenant ordering a repair, the call centre operative has to manually log the repair into the customer relationship management system, and assign a task to a maintenance team to book the engineer.

Channel Shift Survey 2018

If you could pick one digital project for your organisation to start now, what would it be?

Customer self-service	60.15%
Internal systems	21.80%
Website	3.76%
Already in progress	6.02%
Other	8.27%

All of these procedures take too much time. All can be automated. This is what the process of finding a property, signing up and moving in can look like:

How it could be

Step 1

An applicant searches Rightmove on their smartphone for a new home in a different town, finds a property they like the look of – it's a housing association property – and clicks a link which opens a conversation with a Housing Association chatbot.

The chatbot asks for their name, and after asking for a few other details in a quick conversation, informs them that they meet the basic criteria for this property – would they like to apply now? The applicant fills out the application form via their account on the HA's website (it's only 20 questions and takes about 15 minutes) – and finishes by uploading a photo of their ID and proof of right to rent.

Step 2

Some 24 hours later, the applicant receives a notification from the bot, letting them know they've been shortlisted for the property they applied for.

They also get a sample tenancy agreement to read in advance, and are invited to the local community office the next day to undertake a viewing in the Virtual Reality (VR) suite. At the office they do a full viewing with the housing officer via the VR suite – they can walk around the property, get a guided tour of the local streets and amenities, speak to the officer and get a real feel for what it would be like to live there. The applicant decides they'll have a think before making a decision so heads home to sleep on it. They can revisit the property via the website if they wish – there are photos and videos to browse as well as an Augmented Reality (AR) walkthrough that reminds them what it was like being there. The housing officer informs them that the property will be held for them for 24 hours.

Step 3

The next day the applicant decides to go for it – they open the bot and click "accept" – they're asked to view and sign their tenancy agreement using fingerprint or faceID, pay a deposit and select from a series of handover dates to get the keys and move in!

The website also provides really helpful information on moving home – even connecting the user with a local van hire company to help with moving. It also provides checklists and tips for changing address, contact details for local community groups they can get involved with, both before and after they move in, and a secure messaging platform for talking to their new neighbours – it's starting to feel like home and the applicant hasn't even moved in yet!

Step 4

On moving day they're met at the property by the housing officer, who sets them up with a biometric key so they can access their home using their smartphone.

They'll be able to use this to grant access to repairs contractors and friends too – even if they're not home – and see a log of who's been in and out as well. Some of the neighbours they've connected with via the website are there to greet them too, and ready to help them move their stuff into the house – they let their new neighbour know that they can report repairs and pay their rent via the website account now they're a tenant too!

What about the Future?

We know that this smooth process is possible with existing technology, and that the older, time-consuming ways of arranging basic housing services are no longer necessary.

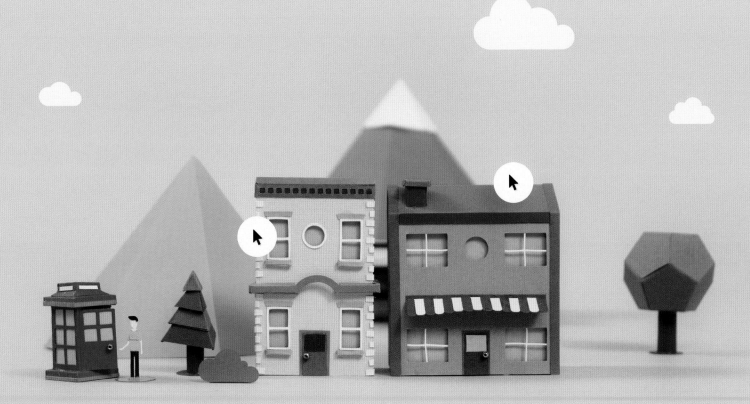

All these routine activities can be made far quicker and easier, for tenant and staff alike, through automation of repeatable tasks and integrating systems to empower tenants to self-serve.

This will provide more work and leisure time for tenants, and enable housing association staff to reduce time on routine queries and transactions, and increase time spent with those with more complex needs. This chapter describes the liberating effects of such an approach – all based on existing technology.

While none of the housing associations featured in our research had achieved the 'perfect' implementation across the range of all services, several have made significant progress, and offer more than a glimpse of the potential for enhancing, even transforming, services and quality of life, and we quote some examples throughout this chapter. We discuss the implementation process in more detail in later chapters. It is more complicated than some envisage, but more doable than many fear.

"

"We are a people business. We always have to give choice in ways of contacting us"

Matt Cooney
Chief Operating Officer, PA Housing

It is about *optimal*, not *maximum*, use of technology, with people and systems working together in harmony. At its core, social housing is a humanitarian movement. Since its foundation, it has existed to alleviate poverty and create decent living standards for people who might otherwise struggle to achieve this. It always will, and always should, retain the direct care from person to person, where this is necessary. But far from diluting this human contact, the smartest uses of technology enhance it. As **Matt Cooney**, Chief Operating Officer at PA Housing, puts it:

"We're a people business, we always have to give choice in contacting us. We have some pretty vulnerable people we provide services to, who really need to phone us, and who need people to advocate on their behalf. I'm very much of the school of thinking that if we have a digital application that works for people, people who want to use it will use it by choice. That takes away a lot of reactive stuff, and provides genuine efficiency, thereby increasing the number of people using that as a result. My personal view is that the telephone will still be highly prevalent in five to ten years' time.

"The choice between phone and digital isn't binary; this or that. If low-level antisocial behaviour issues are done digitally, for example, rather than officers' time dealing with that, there is more time to spend on the serious cases. At the moment, work on benefits is increasingly complex because of Universal Credit – a UC claim is complicated, but it's in our interests to help, because if they can't pay their rent it affects our income."

It would be a mistake to assume that paper-based, telephone or face-to-face modes of contact always provide this human touch more effectively than digital channels can. As Matt indicates, it is common for tenants and staff to experience wasted time and other frustrations with non-digital systems, many of which can be avoided by providing a strong digital offering. For example, a resident may have to set aside time during business hours to undertake a frustratingly long wait attempting to get through to a contact centre simply to pay their rent. Having a platform available to do this online means no waiting on hold during a lunch break – the transaction can be completed at a time or place that suits the tenant. Equally, trained, experienced housing officers may be expected to contact maintenance staff to clean some graffiti, when they would be better employed guiding a vulnerable client through a complicated and stressful benefits application.

Consider the following examples:

'The tap in the bathroom is leaking.'
'There's a light bulb gone in the stairwell.'
'I'm struggling to afford my rent. It's causing me real stress.'

The first two issues here can be swiftly and effectively dealt with through digital channels, freeing the housing officer to deal with the last. At their most advanced, systems can move not only from being reactive to proactive, but can even become predictive, with data used to anticipate issues that are looming as well as those that have already occurred.

Robin Middleton, Head of Digital Marketing at Sovereign Housing, says:

"A smart boiler enables us to remotely diagnose, before a resident even knows there's something wrong. If the sensor is not working, that can be flagged, and [we can] book in a visit from a specialist, and inform the resident that we're sending someone in to check."

Such smart systems ensure continuity of supply of hot water and heating, eliminate wasted time and frustrations for the tenant, and relieve them of the

"

responsibility of monitoring the appliance reliability. They also enhance maintenance and reduce the housing association's costs by enabling repairs to be carried out at an early stage.

The advantages of a well-implemented channel shift programme extend far beyond the matters of more efficient processes and time saved. In our work, reinforced by the research for this book, we have come across examples of tremendous social benefits. You don't have to be a tech giant like Uber or Airbnb to connect people. Housing associations can do this on a local scale, and it can have a transformative effect on estates; it can even help create a safer, more connected and sustainable community. **Paul Taylor**, Innovation Coach at Bromford Housing, has found this to be the case. Their preparation for channel shift was as much anthropological as technological, and some enterprising innovations resulted. He says:

"A lot of housing associations are digitising customer front-end, and withdrawing people; we're doing the opposite. We are digitising transactions but we will have more people than we've ever had, because a number of tests and pilots we did show that if we put more effort into building relationships and connections, and communities, we reduce demand."

"A lot of housing associations are digitising customer front-end, and withdrawing people; we're doing the opposite."

Paul Taylor

Innovation Coach, Bromford Housing

His team spent much time investigating existing service providers and other resources within the community, and put tenants in touch with them. This enabled Bromford to enhance service options to people within the community, without the cost of providing them directly, but rather using digital connections to leverage what was already on offer, and to connect people – fellow housing association tenants and others within the community. In this way, digital connections put potentially isolated people in touch with each other, to get essential services done, share a common interest, or just meet up and have a chat. This reduces their dependence on their landlord, in turn reducing demand and cost for the housing association.

The same healthy dynamics can take place within the workforce, too. This has been the experience at the Rooftop Housing Group. Chief Executive **Boris Worrall** says:

"What we've done is create a modern dynamic digital office environment: hot-desking, new kit. There have been teething problems, but people are mobile, able to work anywhere. It's open plan; people are more collaborative, there is more space for collaboration – to meet, have coffee. It's a different dynamic.

It's given us a platform to say to staff, we're more digital, mobile; that's where we're going to go with customers: take your mobile kit [when you meet them]. At the same time, what we're doing is running workshops and drop-in sessions on the new housing management system.

"In January, we pulled the plug on the old intranet and implemented a workplace social media space like Facebook. It's been a huge success. Many of the staff are using it... they are working in different ways: communicating in forums; [live chats] with each other across teams; celebrating successes, flagging up problems, or just posting that the kitchen is a mess. That's made us a much more digitally savvy organisation, and agile. The principles around digital, and culture, are: open, dynamic, fluid, cross-team... Everything happens there, unfolding in front of you: creative, fluid. That's the default: plus people don't complain that we don't tell you anything, because it's all on here. If you want to know stuff, go look. It's on your phone or your iPad. And people do."

This is an example of cultural change and technological change occurring in step with each other, each supporting the other. Digital connections make team working and communications easier, but

"We give engineers more information in their hands. If they turn up to fix the boiler, they show people how to get online, do other repairs."

Julian Massel
Director of Technology, Trafford Housing Trust

the positive dynamics do not just happen naturally; attention needs to be paid to building a healthy mindset as well as the right technology, as the example at Rooftop shows.

PA Housing has invested in a major transformation programme focused on self-service. The organisation, which was formed in 2017 by the merger of Asra Housing Group and Paragon Housing, has implemented a comprehensive transformation programme implementing digital channel shift.

This programme resulted in a 14% reduction in call volumes year on year within the first year of launch, with 4,700 customers per month accessing the portal, and 10,000 self-service processes completed monthly. The major programme of works included a brand new self-service portal including a full suite of payments workflows and an end-to-end repairs diagnosis, reporting and booking service. This was followed closely by a new-look website centred on self-service.

The self-service portal was initially delivered as a launchpad solution within just 12 weeks in order to consolidate and replicate functionality that was previously spread between multiple other systems through a greatly improved user interface.

Development has continued iteratively since launch, based on both user feedback and user behaviour analysis as well as the needs of the business.

PA Housing has involved stakeholders from across the business throughout this ongoing programme. **Dan Moraga**, Programme Manager for Digital Transformation at PA Housing, has found that by empowering and enthusing staff, engagement and participation by customers has increased as well. He says:

"Colleagues are quite proud [of their knowledge], more recently, as it has improved the quality of service, they are proud to be able to offer something extra to customers; to be able to have a real solution to customers' needs. For example, visiting officers in the past would hear customers say: 'It's difficult to get through to the call centre. We're kept on hold a long time.' This gets our staff thinking about improvements. Now they can say: 'Here, use this website. I'll help you get registered on this, it's really quick and easy.' It does add a real new dimension to people's jobs. Our staff can be a useful test base; we have a wide range of people."

An agile, learning organisation sees itself as growing; it is collectively developing and sharing knowledge every day. Training is not confined to a training department,

and in the context of a housing association, it isn't only the housing officers who help empower the customers. At Trafford Housing Association, for example, repair technicians also help out. **Julian Massel**, Director of Technology at Trafford Housing Trust, says:

"We give engineers more information in their hands. If they turn up to fix the boiler, they show people how to get online, do other repairs. So if the customer hadn't ordered a repair digitally, the engineer would be able to log that s/he showed them how to do so in the future."

The Tenant

I'm a widow with some mobility problems, and I was delighted to be offered a maisonette with a small garden from my local housing association after a while on a waiting list.

It's a few miles from my old home, that I just couldn't cope with anymore. My son bought me an iPad, and while I felt a little intimidated by the technology at first, he soon put me at ease, showed me how to use it, and it was all much easier than I expected.

With help from him and the nice housing officer who met me at the property, I read the tenancy agreement and signed it electronically, and was given access to my tenancy account. It only took a few minutes – quicker than when I did my mortgage application years ago with all those forms. There was already a stock of essential groceries delivered and he showed me how to do the shopping order online for my weekly shop.

I've been invited to join the tenants' association's social media group, and I discovered that there is a quiz on a Thursday evening. I put my name down straight away – I love quizzes. I also discovered a language exchange group, which I joined as I have always wanted to learn Italian. The page also indicates who in the neighbourhood can help with gardening and upholstery. I love gardening, but I can no longer kneel down to pick up weeds, so I arranged for the gardener to do an hour or two each week.

I like the look of the garden, but the geraniums in the pots are starting to get choked. Sorting this out just took a few minutes on the iPad.

My son also told me about the website meetup.com and helped me set up my profile. This was brilliant as I found a book club nearby. I am an avid reader. I can't wait to finish the first book and go to my first meeting.

Meanwhile, the housing officer sent me a friendly welcoming email, offering to help with any needs. As I think I am entitled to Attendance Allowance, I asked for some help with the application. An appointment with the benefits adviser was made for just two days later. The housing officer also showed me how to raise issues through my tenancy account. For example, if there's a nuisance neighbour, I can just report it with a few taps on my iPad. If there's graffiti on my garden fence, I can just take a photo with my iPad and send it, and a few days later someone will come along and sort it.

After only a couple of days in the new home, I felt settled in, and part of a community.

Note: this is a hypothetical case informed by real experiences, but not based on one particular individual

Housing Officer

I was a late convert to smartphones, apps and all things tech. I thought people who spent a lot of time on Facebook were a bit sad; I'd go to a concert or a party in order to enjoy it, not so I could post a picture of it on social media.

I thought that technology was for other people, and that I could concentrate on people, relationships and dealing with social problems.

So when the chief executive of the housing association I work for announced it was going to automate a lot of processes and move us into the twenty-first century, technology-wise, my spirits fell. I envisaged the human touch disappearing, with the poor tenants directed to a soulless list of 'Frequently Asked Questions' on a website, that didn't list the question that they actually wanted to ask, instead of being able to speak to a sympathetic and qualified human being. I was also suspicious of the trend in housing associations to be more commercial, in the light of austerity and changes to the benefits system. Surely this meant cuts to real services, machines replacing people, and social isolation and poverty increasing?

But they won me round, I'll admit through gritted teeth. The IT department showed me that the latest apps and mobile devices are far more user-friendly, versatile and empowering than the web pages of 10-15 years ago and much easier to use than the paper forms I'm used to. They asked me in detail how I spent my day, what my frustrations were, how much wasted activity I became engaged in, and how they could take some of the low-level irritating distractions away from me.

These conversations turned my perceptions of technology upside down. Being honest with them, and with myself, I realised I had probably been spending more than half my working hours on trivial, distracting matters that weren't really core to my job description – like complaints from residents about a boiler not working, or litter in the communal area. In terms of my own admin, internal paper forms – for mileage claims and other expenses, for example – took up a lot of my time, and they promised to reduce the burden there.

What has been the best result of the channel shift project we all went through? Helping keep a vulnerable family safe. I had been aware that K, one of our residents, had been troubled by an aggressive former partner. She had two young children, and was vulnerable. But it didn't seem that there was enough evidence for the police to get involved, there didn't appear to be an imminent threat, and I was so busy with paper forms or minor tenants' issues that I hadn't had the chance to have a longer chat with her.

Once all the residents realised they could get their minor issues dealt with quickly and promptly via a phone or iPad, and I had less bureaucracy too, I found I had a few hours a day to deal with the most sensitive cases, rather than just a few minutes. When I finally had a long chat with K, I discovered with great concern that the threats from her former partner were more severe than I had realised. She had probably been understating them out of not wanting to "make a fuss". I was shocked at the threatening detail in some of his texts, and she showed me the bruises on her upper arm. He would knock on her door or window at any hour of the day or night.

This was enough for me to get the police involved. They sent a specialist officer in domestic abuse cases, and we quickly secured an exclusion order that the former partner actually obeyed. K now breathes a sigh of relief every day and the children are flourishing.

Note: this is a hypothetical case informed by real experiences, but not based on one particular individual

The Advantages

For all the advantages the digital economy can bring, it still generates anxiety. This can be accentuated if the advocates of modernisation overlook legitimate concerns.

Technology exists to alleviate human problems, and its implementation can introduce new risks and challenges while it solves others.

Concerns over personal privacy have increased in recent years, with loss or misuse of personal data by a range of organisations from banks to dating agencies, and concerns over inappropriate use of information harvested by tech giants. This is why the matter of engagement, with staff and with customers, is so important, as it is the route to reassuring and helping people who are not digital natives.

Our experience and research shows that many people have low confidence in their ability to use internet-connected devices; also that in most cases, they are more capable than they believe. So there is a challenge around mindset. In these cases, some guidance and reassurance is the key. Design is also important. If users who are willing to use a device find it too technical or difficult, then it's the solution that is at fault, not the user. The whole purpose of self-service technology is, after all, to make life easier, not more stressful. Housing associations have always held sensitive personal data on their clients, so the challenge is not new, it just has added technical dimensions.

Some of the problems that emerged in our interviews were not to do with the customers, or the technology, but rather with the accuracy and integrity of the data.

Organisations often have multiple platforms, especially if there has been an acquisition or merger. All are working towards the concept of having a single, accurate, continually updated 'version of the truth.' This sounds simple, but can be organisationally difficult in practice – the next chapters will provide guidance on the project management necessary. **Julian Massel**, Director of Technology at Trafford Housing Trust, says they have achieved this single view, but that there is always more to do, and that the discipline required is relentless. He says:

"We now have a single view of the customer and the property; we can start to see all the different interactions. You can take any property, see all the complaints; can look at the person, see the same things. There is still some data cleansing to do. We have done the single view, but that doesn't mean that there aren't gaps – but we can fix those gaps."

Hidden Benefits of Channel Shift

It is not necessarily the case that the latest technology is the best suited for every customer touchpoint. No technology can provide a comforting word when someone is feeling lonely. But it can alert someone with the capacity to help that this need is present, or imminent.

Some consequences of introducing digital connections are unexpected, and many of the unexpected results are benign. **Richard Eden**, Communications Manager at Southway Housing, says digital communication has brought new people into closer contact with officers at the association. He says:

"[Some] people may want to use social media more than they want to call. You go in and assume they'll say: 'We want to speak to someone.' Once you open those platforms up, suddenly you see people contacting you who have never contacted you before; we weren't reaching out just by phone. We're hearing issues that may have been underlying, that

people weren't comfortable discussing in ways that we were offering [before]. So we're reaching out to a different audience."

He has also found that older people are more digitally engaged than expected:

"Actually, they're one of the most active in trying to learn this new world. They attend the classes; know from friends and family, or take it on themselves. I think we've learned a lot more about where the issues come from, or blockages with regards to access. It can be a surprise; not the demographics you expect."

Another positive outcome from our interviews was the evidence that an enhanced customer service, bolstered by optimal use of technology, can help in reducing rent arrears, problems with Universal Credit and even the incidence of repairs needed. This was the initial finding of a pilot scheme at Bromford Housing aimed both at increasing digital communication and developing practical and social skills among tenants, says Innovation Coach **Paul Taylor**:

"What was interesting was that where people had transitioned to Universal Credit [and where they were more connected digitally], we were not showing the same level of arrears as other housing associations. We had bucked the trend of 'This is going to cost us.' What we have shown is that, absolutely, there are efficiencies, in terms of increased financial awareness, even if we thought it was a nice thing to do in terms of getting payments in. We also have evidence of customers needing fewer repairs. The second piece of work is to look at that in more detail. The more we had done in confidence-building, people who can do things for themselves, we pushed on the fact that 'This is your home to look after. We want you to do things yourself.'"

He stresses that, obviously, the association still takes ownership of repairs that are their responsibility, and that can only be done by qualified staff. The point is that encouraging people to be more confident and have more life skills seems to improve confidence and social ability generally, with multiple side-benefits.

These findings represent an encouraging indication that even basic service improvements with optimal use of digital technology can have multiple indirect effects, creating a virtuous circle of happier, more secure and more employable residents paying their rent on time, being less prone to loneliness, mental health problems or anti-social behaviour, reducing their demands on housing officers and other housing association services, freeing up resources to invest in more channel shift initiatives and training for staff and residents.

This chapter presents examples of optimal implementation, not a utopian dream. There will still be challenges in housing management, and crises in people's lives. What this approach does is better equip us to rise to those challenges.

But what if you are a long way from this 'virtuous circle'? How and where to start? The next chapters take you through the processes that have resulted in the benefits described in this chapter. It's not easy; it involves everyone in the organisation. Above all, it is not just about the technology.

03
Describing the steps to progress:
Mindset, Planning, Delivery and Measurement & Improvement

Why is progress towards smart systems, and the kind of optimal use of technology described in the previous chapter, so uneven? Many of the answers lie in the organisation, not the technology. All organisations, ultimately, consist of people, serving other people. Errors abound when forgetting this salient point.

A famous quip of uncertain origin holds that "To err is human. To really foul up you need a computer." But when you investigate apparent technology programme failures in the private or public sectors, it is usually the forms of organisation surrounding the IT system that are dysfunctional, rather than the hardware or software itself. The thoroughly researched book *The Blunders of Our Governments* by Ivor Crewe and Anthony King looked at dozens of failed public policy programmes, many featuring new IT systems and costing billions of pounds in waste. The authors discovered that the real failures lay in: ignorance by planners of how people live their lives, a tendency to neglect training of key personnel, and a naïve belief that the latest IT system will automatically make processes more efficient, including in dysfunctional organisations. In other words, the failures are human – to do with judgement, forms of organisation, levels of training, and communication.

Understanding this essential point is but a first step, however. Actual implementation towards the optimal state is tough, involving thousands of hours of laborious work cleansing data, integrating IT systems, training individuals and service users on technology, and tweaking the design of an app in response to feedback (almost no new service is just right the first time it goes live). Sometimes, tough decisions need to be made about closing down previous forms of communication, and reassigning and retraining staff to operate the new services.

As **Paul Earnden**, Director, Prodo, puts it: "Simplicity is an advantage that has to be constantly sought. Usually things do start simply, but over time, complexity has a tendency to creep in, often to help resolve a short-term issue. But you cannot add simplicity in, you have to constantly look to take complexity out – it takes a strong cultural mindset and courage to fight for it."

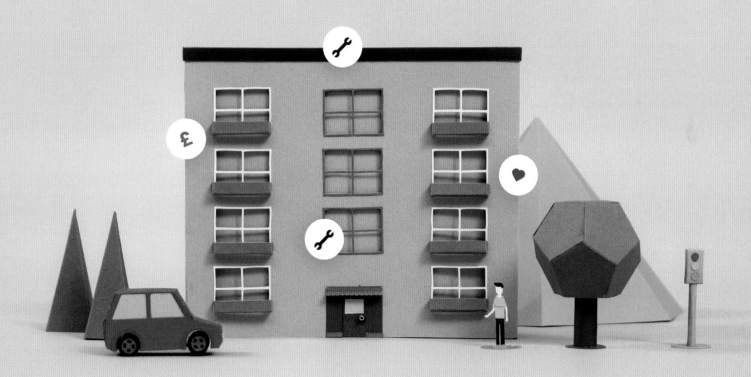

Modernisation of communications

In our experience, successful moves towards the modernisation of communications and systems in social housing have involved four key steps, which must all be attended to, and in the correct order, to achieve effective project management.

We devote this chapter to describing this approach, and the stages involved, as it is a radical break from that which many managers have grown up with. Subsequent chapters take the reader through each stage in turn.

1. Mindset

Understanding mindset, culture and existing ways of working.

2. Planning

Using the intelligence and understanding of mindset and organisational dynamics gathered in Phase 1. This data and qualitative information is used to create an architectural plan of the channel shifts needed, and how and when they can be implemented.

3. Delivery

Delivery against the plan, with flexibility to adapt to circumstances. Train all individuals in the new systems, and gather feedback continually from staff and service users to inform ongoing iterations of apps, portals, etc.

4. Measure

Measure and improve services in response to feedback.

"Some organisations try to find the utopian channel shift; really, you need to be focused on what can be delivered quickly."

Ivo Kerkhof
Head of Strategy, Prodo Digital

Housing associations involved in channel shift are increasingly adopting an agile, team-based, and innovative approach. **Steve Dungworth,** Director of Digital Transformation at Accent Housing, describes how the organisation has a multi-disciplinary Transformation Board, comprising senior stakeholders and executives. "We talk about strategic direction and risk management. We also ensure that the process owners [are involved]: the experts are involved in the project teams, which involve not only the IT disciplines, but different parts of the business; change managers; the voice of the customer; taking actions, communications, testing, training."

Innovative companies are characterised by continual experimentation and iteration; by "permission to fail", provided constructive lessons are learned. This is a marked change from the more cautious traditional culture of housing associations. You don't have to build the perfect solution first time. It is often more effective, as part of an innovative culture based on continuous improvement, to start with a launchpad that has relatively basic functionality (Minimum Viable Product, or MVP) and to build upon that, based on measurement of and feedback from customers/users. Technology is always developing too, so working this way allows you to build in new technologies post-launch rather than going live with a 'perfect' solution that's technologically out of date.

Ivo Kerkhof, Head of Strategy at Prodo, says:

"Some organisations try to find the utopian channel shift; really, you need to be focused on what can be delivered quickly – a minimum viable starting point, delivered early, so you can then learn and iterate. Partly this is because the technology is shifting all the time and partly because you can get buy in and feedback faster."

Awareness of mindset, and the importance of testing and intelligence-gathering, are disciplines that are essential throughout a channel shift programme. Such an approach supports great planning. It creates a broad, evidence-based foundation for a coherent plan, and helps identify the end goals, and ensure that they are based on customers' needs. The plan identifies who is responsible, what the risks are, when the key milestones should be reached, the measures of success, and the communication required pre- and post- each key stage. The Delivery phase, in turn, is highly participative, and evidence-based. It may involve events, road trips, digital champions; different ways of bringing people together to spread the knowledge about new channels and how they can improve quality of life for tenants. The communications team has a significant role, but also new technology such as Virtual Reality. Gamification – creating fun activities with incentives to nudge people towards channel shift – can also play a part. Information-sharing works both ways, with feedback from customers informing planners with ideas for design tweaks. Such interaction continues into the fourth phase, Measurement & Improvement.

Mindset is critical. It seems like an indulgence to some, but the biggest problems in implementation arise from short-cutting or omitting this essential discipline. As discussed in Chapter 1, the conventional business model of the last century is increasingly regarded as no longer fit for purpose in a digitally connected, fast-changing economy. It featured a top-down approach in an institution structured into specialist departments, rather than project teams; change programmes that were imposed, where employee participation was low, and technological upgrades were owned and run by the IT department. This approach has been exposed as too rigid, too compartmentalised, and too slow.

It follows from this that the approach to successful project management, as part of channel shift and improved employee engagement and customer service, is radically different in an agile business model. It would be a mistake, however, to imagine that the process is less ordered, or the planning less rigorous. ***There isn't less planning. There is more involvement.*** This often means a slower start to the process than a top-down approach, as time and effort are expended to understand the culture, educate people about

change and engage them in the enterprise. The reward is much smoother roll-out, fewer implementation problems, more engaged and empowered staff, and happier customers. Where problems arise – technical glitches, customer portals that are not user-centric, problems with quality of data – those involved in the project become aware of them earlier, and have buy-in from others involved, and a shared resolve to tackle the problems.

The first step in the new approach to change management in digital modernisation programmes has little to do with technology or even management – at least management in the conventional sense of being concerned only with tasks and deadlines. It's about *understanding*: the current ways of working, the mindset and culture of all those involved – employee, customer, partners. It involves testing common assumptions or hypotheses – such as 'people hate change'. Before reaching an understanding of how processes, relationships and connections can be improved, it is essential to know how they currently function. There may be healthy patterns to retain and enhance, as well as wasteful procedures that can be replaced. Moreover, this discipline of healthy inquiry, hypotheses-testing and monitoring is ideally maintained throughout a channel shift project, and after (see page 61).

This idea that the IT function shouldn't be the only lead role in a technological upgrade is a challenge to many conventional management approaches. The function obviously has a leading role, but it is most effective when this is leadership-in-partnership. This was the biggest lesson in channel shift for **Rich Harvey**, Head of IT at Housing Solutions. He recalls:

"What we were quite bad at was leading stuff from the IT point of view. IT had the lead on different projects – that's why people were not as accepting – rather than coming from the business. It felt 'pushed' by IT. So we tried to change. There was a bit of anger to IT projects, not anger just a bit of hostility. When we spent more time with them, and they could see the benefits, they were happy with a mixture of both."

With hindsight, he and his colleagues learned that they should have been looking at the processes more from a customer's point of view, and spent more time ensuring that alternatives to phoning the call centre offered a better service; also, that the benefits were explained more fully to customers, such as the ease of requesting a repair online. "We are switching more towards asking customers: 'You tell us what you want, and we will find an IT solution.'"

Towards an Agile Approach – Key Features

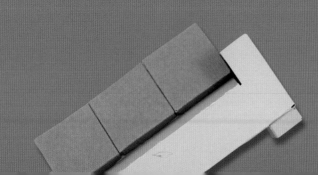
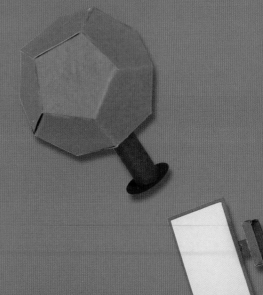

Agile Approach
Key Features

Conventional Corporation	Agile Company
CEO and IT function design and control change programme	Multi-disciplinary teams co-create project management
Limited gathering of organisational intelligence or testing of assumptions	Comprehensive data-gathering. Hypothesis-testing
Intelligence held by the elite	Intelligence shared widely
Roll-out to central design and timetable	Flexible implementation, learning lessons along the way
Assumption that people are hostile to change	Assumption that people will engage with change, though may require training and support
Focus on deadlines and financial KPIs	Continual monitoring and measurement, combining qualitative and financial measures
Quest for the 'perfect' design	Rapid innovation and implementation, continual iteration

"

"Getting the right people at the right time, rather than a unilateral decision, bringing people along on the journey..."

Jenny Bradshaw
Group Account Director, Prodo Digital

Jenny Bradshaw, Group Account Director at Prodo, says:

"Starting with the end in mind is key. Having that need rooted in real benefits and positive outcomes is going to be the key to success. It's very easy to sit in a boardroom and think what the right approach is, but you need evidence; talk to customers, stakeholders. Use different tools to generate insights into existing customer behaviours; what customers are inquiring about, and identifying ways we can successfully channel shift certain things through a new solution, getting the right people at the right time, rather than a unilateral decision, bringing people along on the journey: staff, customers."

One caveat when describing this more participative approach is that it should not be seen as a means of indefinitely postponing difficult decisions or fudging leadership and managerial responsibilities. Technological change doesn't necessarily mean widescale redundancies; it is more common that roles change rather than disappear. Sometimes, however, some posts do become redundant – some call centre roles, those managing the cash desk, and so on. Many individuals can be reassigned, but this is not always possible. Leadership towards the *Shift* in an agile organisation still involves the core disciplines of planning, deadlines, and making tough decisions. But by being more informed, participative, adaptive and innovative, the new ways of working are likely to result in projects that are better planned and better accepted within the community the organisation is serving, and the staff team responsible for delivery.

The four stages summarised in this chapter, Mindset, Planning, Delivery and Measurement & Improvement, are empirically established, having supported successful channel shift initiatives in numerous organisations. The next four chapters take us through the key disciplines in more detail.

04
Mindset:
Understand the organisation, change the mindset

In the previous chapter, we discussed how change programmes that are led and dominated by technology considerations, with minimal involvement of customers and the wider employee population, have a poor track record.

An engaging and team-based way of project management is more effective, and is in keeping with the agile business model of the twenty-first century. Before implementing channel shift, it's important to understand what the current patterns of interaction, attitudes to technology and organisational ability to adapt are, so that the plan develops from the existing reality as a foundation. If the organisation's mindset is indifferent or resistant to adopting new communication channels, even if only in parts of the business, then this needs acknowledging and shifting.

Channel Shift Survey 2018

45%: little to no confidence in their organisation's ability to procure and implement the right channel shift solutions on budget and on time.*

Another dimension is that an organisation's mindset is not hermetically sealed from the society that surrounds it. Rather, it is shaped and influenced by it. The societal culture around digital technology is in a state of considerable flux; mobile connected devices are almost ubiquitous at the time of writing, and further disruptive innovations are constant. An approach to channel shift based on an assumption that the organisation is technologically ahead of the customer base and has to push or cajole customers along, may be out of date for some organisations in a society where people routinely book holidays, look for properties and pay bills on their mobile.

There is an increasing expectation of all organisations, even if they're not Amazon or the BBC, that you will be using technologies in a way that consumers are comfortable with. Increasingly, it's seen as a reflection of the organisation, from a brand point of view, and how you care. People are making decisions about you across multiple areas. Every touchpoint tells your customer about your organisation. If your touchpoints don't match your organisation's mindset, you've got a mismatch straight away.

* Because of negative past experiences with similar projects, lack of buy in or lack of strategic direction.

Of course, while understanding and shifting the mindset is essential preparation to channel shift, in practice this discipline takes place in parallel with development of the technology. Going live with unreliable software or poorly designed apps can cause a serious setback in the acceptance of new communication channels.

Channel Shift Survey 2018

89% aware that their organisation has channel shift objectives.

79% know what those objectives are

Some of the interviewees in our research emphasised the importance of rigorous testing before going live, though many also stressed that you don't always have to wait for the system to be 'perfect' – just reliable enough to be operational, while tech teams work continuously on new iterations in response to feedback. The opposite, however, is also the case: an excellent product design and infrastructure may not be adopted in an organisation where people are suspicious of new technology, fearful of redundancies, or where trust is low for a range of reasons.

This parallel development of developing IT systems, gathering organisational intelligence, and nurturing a high-engagement mindset, comes naturally in an atmosphere where collaboration levels are high and project planning is multi-disciplinary. The optimal mindset for channel shift is more than just readiness to use mobile devices; it also refers to the organisational climate more generally, in line with the agile, high-engagement workplace discussed in earlier chapters. The most effective channel shift projects take place in organisations where there are high levels of healthy communication and cooperation.

Channel Shift Survey 2018

58% feeling little to no involvement in hitting channel shift objectives

But how does shifting the mindset work in practice? The social housing sector is by no means at the beginning of this initiative, and there are some valuable examples on practical implementation. This chapter offers a practical guide based on these experiences. It is divided into two sections: *Understand the mindset* and *Shift the mindset*.

Understand the Mindset

Developing an understanding of mindset under a broad definition, referring to engagement and working environment as well as readiness for using digital communication, means that organisations need to gather both qualitative and quantitative intelligence. You need conversations, interviews, questionnaires and observations as well as data.

The hard data will tell you much about what is happening – use of the telephones, efficiency of resolution of issues, changes in channels over time. The qualitative information will tell you more about why: if morale is low, or teamwork is patchy, or there is reluctance to use certain means of communication because of reliability issues or lack of training.

Channel shift is at least as much about mindset change as technological change. **Claire Bayliss**, consultant at 3C Consultants, observes:

"In many ways, it's probably *more* about a culture change. Technology is only an enabler. It's all about that business process, yet the culture change is maybe the hardest part. Sorting technology is straightforward; making it successful, that's difficult."

This is an observation shared by **Brian Halligan**, CEO of the global marketing automation firm, Hubspot. He says that "much of this change is as much mindset as it is technology. In the 1990s, sales and marketing

were intensely people heavy. In the past fifteen years, there's been a huge investment in technologies – CRM, content marketing, marketing automation – to increase the productivity of customer-facing employees. The big shift now is to increase 'customer productivity,' where customers are largely interacting with systems and software, and only interacting with actual people at key specific points in the process. For growing organisations, that means they need to place less of a premium on specialists within organisational silos, and instead hire for and train for customer-facing staff who can not only go deep, but also go wide and perform functions across multiple disciplines."

A commonly heard phrase in business has been that 'people hate change.' We challenge this assumption. Given that human beings are naturally curious and hungry for news, it was always a surprising claim, and it has not been our experience, in the numerous successful channel shift projects that we have been involved in, and in the interviews for this book. We find that housing officers or a grandmother in a sheltered housing project, are often very keen for change. They are happy to use an iPad for connecting with colleagues, or ordering a repair, provided the system is well designed, they understand how and why they should use it, and are reassured that connections are secure.

What people hate is not change in itself, but being disempowered and uninformed. This relates to staff and customers alike.

In terms of *organisational mindset*, understanding the community you are serving, and above all its diversity, is essential intelligence when

> **"In many ways, it's probably more about a culture change. Technology is only an enabler."**
>
> **Claire Bayliss**
> 3C Consultants

preparing for channel shift. So is working in teams. IT professionals, and those with responsibility for HR and organisational development, need to work closely together, so that the people, the teams and the technology roll-out are designed and implemented in an integrated way.

Another factor that is sure to grow as the demographics of the customer base change, is the different ways of working, communicating and socialising that digital natives have compared with older generations. Younger people are less wedded to the nine-to-five routine, and like to dip into and out of work. They may wish to work any hour or socialise any hour, in our experience, and that of some of our interviewees. This means that they are temperamentally well suited to the agile business model described in earlier chapters, featuring rapid innovation, experimentation and iteration, by teams that are digitally connected most of the time. Those who were schooled in slower, more formal methods of business planning could potentially learn lessons from their newer recruits.

Digital readiness of customers is another key dimension. Some of our interviewees carried out surveys on this, and a number were surprised by the results. **Matt Cooney**, Chief Operating Officer at PA Housing, says: "It's a decreasing minority of people [who are internet refuseniks]. When we checked – we did a survey three years ago, things will have moved on – we knew that for certain 73% of our customers had used the internet in some form or other, typically on a smartphone. If you can deliver functionality to that level of user experience, that's where you need to be."

A survey at Housing Solutions unearthed the finding that the telephone system was almost too effective; call centre staff answered quickly and were helpful, customers were very happy with the service. It was free to customers, and 80% of calls were answered within 20 seconds, says **Rich Harvey**, Head of IT at the association. This was a contrast with some other housing associations, where tenants sometimes experienced waiting times before getting through on the telephone. It posed a challenge for Housing Solutions in terms of switching channel away from a popular means of communication to a cheaper, more efficient one; there was an extra incentive to make the new system very highly effective. The advantage of such a starting point, however, was high levels of customer engagement and satisfaction, providing a foundation for change.

Dan Moraga, Programme Manager for Digital Transformation at PA Housing, reports that his most important recent lesson on the digital programme was to include a wide range of stakeholders in groundwork necessary to understand the customer base. Issues of self-awareness also emerged in the research. "There is a real range: from 'No, I've never been online and I never want to use it, I want to speak to someone,' to: 'Get me signed up. I never want to talk to you,' and everyone in between. Our initial market research revealed big demand, but a poor level of education. We sent out a huge survey; 15-16,000 customers. We got just under 3,000 responses, many returned by email. One question was: do you use the internet? Some said no, but returned by email!"

> **"What people hate is not change, but being disempowered"**

Shift the Mindset

Shifting the mindset to enable channel shift could be narrowly defined in terms of the 'nudge' required to incentivise people to switch from phone calls to an app. There is much discussion in many housing associations about limiting use of the phone, or offering a better service online – for example, the ability to specify a precise time for an appointment for a repair engineer.

While incentives and nudges play a role, they are best supported by a deeper commitment to preparing people, using digital champions, social media, training days and other events. Office and workplace design may require attention, too. It may be all very well to talk about a digitally connected, agile organisation, but if the senior executives are in closed-off offices, rarely chat with other staff, and don't prioritise use of digital media in their own communications, then progress will be stymied. The challenge of mindset needs addressing at all levels, not just digital preparedness of customers.

At Rooftop Housing, efforts have been made to 'supercharge' mindset shift, in the term used by Chief Executive **Boris Worrall**. This involved providing people with the right equipment, and changing both ways of working and attitudes to digital technology, with the aim of "creating an environment where we're mobile, digital and agile." He says:

"You can't expect people to be able to deliver a great digital service when you don't have your staff doing that on a day-to-day basis. So we implemented new kit, flexible working, and a mobile office environment. That's changing the way people think, act, behave and work. At the same time, we've bought a new housing management system. That's enabling us to improve the customer interface: so what you cannot do is simply tell people you're going online if you don't have the platform. You can't nudge until you have a really good alternative… You can then start to think about how to nudge. This is controversial, but you can make it a bit more difficult to phone us; restricted office hours. The idea there is that you make it easier to interact."

In January 2018, Rooftop replaced its old intranet with a more interactive social media space for staff, which has been "a huge success." He adds:

"They are working in different ways: communicating in forums; live chats with each other across teams; celebrating successes, flagging up problems, or just posting that the kitchen is a mess. That's made us a much more digitally savvy organisation, and agile. The principles around digital, and culture, are: open, dynamic, fluid, cross-team."

Mindset shift is a leadership role. The organisations that succeed tend to feature a clear lead from the C-suite. Often, we come across individuals in marketing roles with strong ideas and a clear vision of how channel shift can improve quality of life, and how it can be implemented, but without support from the top of the organisation, it is an uphill struggle.

> ## "You can't expect people to be able to deliver a great digital service when you don't have your staff doing that on a day-to-day basis."
>
> **Boris Worrall**
> Rooftop Housing

For all the considerable discussion around changing the mindset within staff and customers, there is sometimes an even bigger challenge: updating the mindset of business leaders. In the previous chapter we critiqued the common assumption in change programmes that 'people hate change.' As discussed, it's far from a general truth, but resistance to change can be encountered – and sometimes those most resistant are precisely those who should be leading the change.

There have been numerous examples in recent years of business leaders who have been slow to react to change. Often, the change is caused in large part by technological change – internet-based disruptors were a factor in the demise of large retailers such as Woolworths and Toys R Us. Typically, it is not the technology itself, but more an understanding of the complex dynamics of how markets change, that is key to being able to adapt. An important point to note is that some established firms, including very old businesses, have so far adapted and continued to thrive. Some have set up successful entrepreneurial new ventures, such as Nestlé with Nespresso. The difference lies in the agility and inventiveness of the firm, not its age.

Housing associations traditionally have a hands-on relationship with their customers, which is distinct from the digital culture which involves the concept of self-help. Obviously, the most dependent tenants will always need a lot of support, but there are many tenants who are not only able to sort out the logistics of rent, repair and so on, but feel liberated in being able to do so for themselves.

There is a real challenge there, internally and operationally, in terms of moving away from the mindset of hand-holding customers, towards enabling customers to do more for themselves.

Orbit Housing has engaged in a "massive" focus on staff and customer engagement, as it moved away from a local authority mindset, says **Kevin Hornsby**, Head of Tenancy Sustainment at the association. There is an ambition to be recognised as one of the Top 100 companies to work for. Improving employee engagement, and making technological channel shift, are part of the same broader strategic change. He adds:

"When we work on projects, we want to engage staff and embed it... Staff engagement is critical. It is really important to get motivation: ideas, thoughts; also landing it, in terms of outcome. We had a team of [digital] champions, working nationally, providing local information."

To an extent, there is a natural evolution in demographics towards a population that is at ease with digital technology, certainly as users. The 'old' perceived divide between techies and other disciplines has diminished as the use of mobile devices and digital connections becomes ubiquitous. Several of our interviewees noted that digital resistance was breaking down to a certain degree through staff turnover, as digital natives from Generation Z enter the workforce. This natural evolution does require acceleration, however, with the help of the initiatives mentioned in this chapter: digital champions, training courses, setting up internal social media pages, and so on, but there is a favourable wind.

> **"Staff engagement is critical. It is really important to get motivation. "**
>
> **Kevin Hornsby**
> Orbit Housing

Steve Dungworth, Head of Digital Transformation at Accent Housing, indicates that there can still be something of a cultural divide between IT people, traditionally typecast as being insular or too 'nerdy,' and those in relationship-based professions. This concept of a divide may be becoming dated, however, in the younger generation. He says:

"In IT we like technology, but the people at Accent are there to serve customers – they are passionate about that… When we start talking techy language, it can turn them off. People and technology don't always mix. By the same token, IT people are not always the best at engaging. But I have recruited good IT people with strong communication skills. We call them T-shaped people, and it is surprisingly not difficult. We are looking for attitude, social skills. The first couple of people I recruited were apprentices, young people. They went down a storm with our customers – great empathy, great understanding; wasn't always about the technology."

This policy of blending technological upgrades and digital training with attention to building a positive mindset and culture is a characteristic of what we have experienced in successful channel shifts. Concepts such as culture and mindset can sound nebulous when discussed in an abstract way, but there is no doubting their immense power when you are operating in a dynamic, highly engaged workplace, with a clear vision and a lead from the top of the organisation. Everything becomes possible.

Learning points around mindset

- Make sure the business's leaders are living the mindset change, by being digitally connected, and also open and communicative

- Don't make assumptions around people's readiness for channel shift; it may be higher than you think. There is also likely to be a broad spectrum of attitudes among tenants, and the staff population

- Gather data and conduct surveys to find out the reality in the organisation. Don't rely on common narratives or guesswork

- Encouraging use of social media internally by staff and residents, for example with Facebook pages or an organisation's own platform, can encourage mindset change and digital familiarity simultaneously.

05
Planning:
The collective mindset and organisational culture

While the collective mindset and the organisational culture are being primed, planning your channel shift project can begin in earnest. The twin disciplines are best seen as closely related and complementary, rather than discrete and separate.

The best plans combine tangible targets with attention to improving culture and a roadmap for how they can be delivered. For example, the goal may be 70% channel shift within three years, but with an understanding that effort will need to be expended on training, communication and other ways of improving organisational climate in order to achieve that. If understanding and changing mindset is about the who and the why, planning involves the what, the how and the when.

This means setting out a clear roadmap for change, with itemised actions, and people assigned to those, allowing for clear accountability and no ambiguity. An approximate rule of thumb is whether the senior team can articulate their vision to an outside party. If they can, they are usually well on the way to success, with only teething troubles and other obstacles along the way.

Know the Territory

Continuing with the route planning metaphor, in order to have a usable roadmap, you need to know the territory: the starting point and the desired end point.

Core to the planning process, then, is detailed, forensic examination of current patterns of communication and organisational dynamics. **Robin Middleton** Head of Digital Marketing at Sovereign Housing, says:

"We looked at what currently is creating heavy use of resources within our business model and what can be relatively simply transferred online, and developed a matrix:

A   Is there a big workload? Offline? Lots of inbound calls? Correspondence? A lot of people going out to interact with our customers?

B   How simple is that to be implemented online?

"That matrix highlights which solutions are most cost-effective."

As an example, the ability for a resident to request to have a pet in their property would seem to be a personal request, best suited for the telephone. Yet it is possible that the inquiry can be handled online, given the clear rules Sovereign has, and the data it holds, he says.

"We know your property; we know if you have a private garden; all of that information. We can give a relatively instant decision. We have our own internal rules about dogs, cats, and so on. We can build that knowledge."

Making decisions on when face-to-face or with telephone-based contact still forms a part of the research. The project team at Sovereign held in-depth conversations to discuss all the different interactions that could be put into a portal, and supported this with detailed analysis. If face-to-face interaction was more appropriate – in order to maintain a relationship or because the matter was too subtle and nuanced to be automated – then it came lower down the priority list for automation, or reserved for direct conversation.

The discipline required here is, once accurate intelligence is gathered on existing use of communications channels, to be able to take a step back and ask: if the organisation were being designed afresh, with all modern technology available, how much of that interaction would be through old media, such as phone calls or face-to-face meetings? In practice, it may be relatively little – but where communications do need to be more personal, it may be important to retain the human touch. Such analysis forms the basis of the channel shift plan. As discussed in earlier chapters, the purpose of the channel shift is not dispassionately automating every process, but rather to enhance quality of life for tenants. Switching communications technology to newer media is only done with this aim in mind.

"An approximate rule of thumb is whether the senior team can articulate their vision to an outside party"

Trafford Housing set up a Transformation Team, and one of its tasks was to work closely with the technical team to map the existing patterns of communication. According to **Julian Massel**, Director of Transformation, this turned up inefficiencies in internal processes, too.

"There were too many touch-points, too many people involved, too much waiting. On matters such as repairs, reporting antisocial behaviour, and so on. For example, you would phone up and you would wait for someone to call you back. Digital technology is going to solve that... We're looking at dynamic routing; available slots when there's an engineer going past that area. Amazon have been doing this for years. There may be non-urgent repairs, but an engineer will be in your area Friday. We can ask 'How does that suit you?' You couldn't do that on the phone."

Such ingenuity, building on innovations made in other sectors, can help housing providers enhance services, particularly around more convenient arrangements for repairs. Channel shift can offer far more than streamlining existing processes.

PA Housing carried out a large survey, covering customers and other appropriate parties. This informed the digital strategy that underpinned their transformation programme. Once the strategy was approved, it was handed over to the Project Management Office that works on most of the large corporate change projects at the business. **Dan Moraga**, Programme Manager for Digital Transformation at PA Housing, says:

"It's such a diverse customer base, some with high levels of need, and requiring support. Yet the demand for digital services is still strong. For us to be able to work with our partners, and design effective processes that nudge behaviour away from face-to-face to get them to call us, and then to encourage self-service or website or digital channel, you have to make sure it appeals to a wide range of people."

Several interviewees referred to learning from digital companies, online banks and others who are further along the digital transformation journey. In the case of Orbit Housing, the prompt for a major Shift towards digital systems came from front-line staff, recommending that many processes could move to being online, says **Kevin Hornsby**, Head of Tenancy Sustainment at the association. The Project Management Team took up the challenge in 2015. To accelerate and inform the process, team members looked at what some organisations in other sectors were doing, that were further advanced, including insurance companies and the DVLA.

Some housing associations have modelled themselves on young innovative companies, in order to seek the blend of mindset shift closely integrated with smart planning. Bromford Housing Association set up an Innovation Lab, modelled on start-up digital companies. "It was set up to answer the question: who owns the bright ideas in the organisation?" says **Paul Taylor**, Innovation Coach.

The result was a multi-disciplinary team that committed itself to renewing the organisation and its technology. "It involves a diverse group

"We need a single version of the truth. It needs to be single and it needs to be the truth"

of people, rather than just a few people at the top of the organisation – sometimes, more challenging. When we started Innovation Lab, we did a pitch to the then CEO. We wanted a small amount of resource, we acknowledged that 70% of ideas will fail; the concept of allowable failure wasn't culturally acceptable at the time. They totally bought into that and got behind it, aware that the 30% would be good, and we would evidence the learning from the stuff that failed. We found we were pushing at an open door."

He adds that innovation "is a massively over-used word, usually misapplied. There are at least three crucial stages: the idea, the vision, which is the easy bit; the second part is doing something, moving on it; and the third is the added value, to internal processes or to the customer. Often people refer to it as the idea bit, rather than the execution... innovation is ultimately a process."

As discussed in Chapter 3, a more participative approach to project management, in an agile company, involves just as much rigorous planning as in a more hierarchical organisation. There has to be project management leadership, with named individuals for key tasks, and accountability right through the process. Businesses that implement change projects really well, both in housing and non-housing sectors, typically have someone in an overarching role, usually with either a technical or sales and marketing background, with a job title like Digital Transformation Officer. They have taken the trouble to understand the legacy systems that you may have.

Richard Eden, Communications Manager at Southway Housing, says: "Everyone is involved in the planning. We have a digital strategy, created through a senior management team and general management, run by all staff. Everyone is now accountable for it. That strategy has an action plan, it led to the creation of the post of Digital Inclusion Officer. We're accountable to the board on that. It's at the highest level of planning. At a practical level, it feeds into systems, and there's an action plan for every team."

Accent Housing has a busy contact centre, with live call data, such as numbers in the queue, average waiting time and so on, displayed on a screen. It has a clearly defined target established at the planning stage. The aim was to make the online alternatives sufficiently attractive that they will be overwhelmingly preferred. **Steve Dungworth,** Director of Digital Transformation at Accent, acknowledges that difficult decisions may have to be taken later in the digital transition, should the phone option continue to be popular. Running parallel services could be popular, but expensive:

"We have 22,000 properties, and 37,000 residents contacting us on a regular basis. That's why we have a contact centre. We know that 80% of residents contact us by phone, for rent or repairs. Nothing surprising about that. We set ourselves an aspiration that it would be 50% online by 2020. That seems doable. The reason for moving to online is to improve customer service, to create more choice. Here's the rub: more choice, with a brilliant website, will drive channel shift, but if we just add more choice, we could be paying for everything twice."

"In order to have a usable roadmap, you need to know the territory"

One of the key considerations is to acknowledge at the planning stage that there will have to be flexibility. This comes naturally to the agile organisation. A project plan for modernising communications channels in human interactions has to be more dynamic and fluid than, say, an architect's plan for a bridge or a building. This is for several reasons: the customer base will be diverse, each organisation is unique, customers will produce unexpected feedback – informing you, for example, that the portal doesn't present so well on a specific mobile device, or that a list of repairs options is incomplete. Another factor is that communications technology is changing all the time. Some technologies may change in the course of a few months or even become obsolete in a couple of years, so flexibility has to be built in. In the largest, most complex projects, it's advisable to have a Plan B. In all digital transformation projects, the smartest way is to continually implement, experiment, gain feedback and iterate.

A key way to help ensure smooth transition is to involve customers at the planning stage. This has been a point of learning for many of the companies involved in channel shift. It helps the project managers adapt and be responsive. **Matt Cooney**, Chief Operating Officer at PA Housing, says: "We didn't involve customers enough in the first wave, that's why we've had to make revisions to the customer experience. We now test everything with customers; invite them in, manually, face-to-face, get direct feedback from them... It's always better to have customers with you, so you get a proper insight into what they mean by their comments."

Where planning segues into implementation is in the laborious discipline of data cleansing and creation of a single database, a 'single version of the truth.' It needs to be single and it needs to be the truth. In all our work, and in the experience of our interviewees, this is essential, as there are obvious, and potentially very serious, setbacks if errors on the database lead to repair requests that aren't logged, maintenance staff turning up at the wrong address, and so on. It is an obvious point, and seems straightforward, but it can be a time-consuming task, requiring skilled project management, as many organisations have multiple systems that need integrating. Typically, there are separate legacy systems for finance, customer relationship management, the property database and so on. If there has been a merger, the number increases proportionally. Switching to a single database, carefully checking for accuracy, and ensuring all new data is correct, are considerable tasks.

Julian Massel, Director of Technology at Trafford, says: "We have a single customer record; we will be able to do business intelligence and data analysis tools. Now we're going to launch a digital customer online [service]. The missing link is workflow automation, and then we will have cracked it."

> **"We didn't involve customers enough in the first wave, that's why we've had to make revisions to the customer experience."**

Matt Cooney
PA Housing

Practical planning steps

When planning a typical channel shift project, it's helpful to cover a number of areas to ensure that the project is successful.

We conclude this chapter with a practical guide to the key planning steps necessary. As with any major project, the planning stage will be lengthy and considered, and the project will only take place if the organisational mindset is in the right place, as discussed in earlier chapters.

1.

Set up a Digital Project Management Group

Successful projects typically gather a team of stakeholders from across the business and from all levels of the business to drive the project forward, communicate progress back to the business and represent their areas within the project. These groups meet regularly, are chaired by a Director or board member and are involved with every aspect of the project, from procurement of suppliers right through to delivery and measurement.

This group is the team who will be responsible for making the project happen – so they need to be motivated, engaged and bought into the process. Most importantly, they should be guided by the overall objectives of the project and the needs of the organisation first, and their own personal business areas second.

2.

Managing & mitigating risk

Appointed suppliers and external consultants should be invited to join these groups too. This is an opportunity for them to report progress but also to bring along new ideas, challenge decisions and inform with experience from other projects.

Once the management / steering group is set up you would want to establish clear communication channels. Obviously one of those would be the regular group meetings but in between you can use email, Slack, Skype or some other tool as your means to communicate as a group. You can share documents using tools like Microsoft OneDrive, Google Drive or Dropbox, which provide a secure and simple way of working together simultaneously in real time.

Building a risk mitigation plan helps you respond quickly to issues during delivery.

This is a simple but critically important document that all stakeholders need to be aware of and agree as early as possible. In essence, it's a list of anything that could negatively impact or derail the project. For each of these risks, you need to add:

* **A grading to indicate respectively both severity and likelihood**
* **Who is responsible for resolving / managing**
* **Description of the risk**
* **The impact of the risk on the project, in line with the severity grading**
* **The response to the risk**

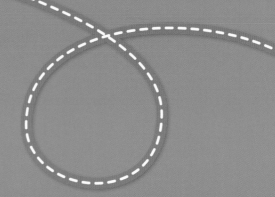

A RACI chart will help establish who needs to be involved at key stages of the project and who is responsible for what. A RACI chart is simply a matrix of all activities or decisions, with individuals assigned as either Responsible, Accountable, Consulted or Informed for each one.

Responsible: person who performs an activity or does the work

Accountable: person who is ultimately accountable and has Yes/No/Veto

Consulted: person who needs to feedback and contribute to the activity

Informed: person who needs to know of the decision or action

Within this RACI – assigning key points of contact is a useful discipline, both for you internally and for third parties. From a supplier's point of view, it's always easier to have a single point of contact for feedback, amendments and general project coordination, particularly when there are multiple stakeholders to be consulted on both sides. All of this can be set out and agreed in a project initiation meeting, which involves

everyone who will have a part in delivering the project (including third parties). This will help ensure the project gets off on the right foot and that everyone is on the same page in terms of what's being delivered.

Channel Shift Survey 2018

What tend to be the biggest blockers to digital projects or initiatives making it through planning to actual delivery?

IT system limitations	**41.26%**
Time and/or resources	**20.00%**
Disagreements across departments and/or conflicts with other projects	**18.05%**
Budgets	**7.32%**
Other	**13.16%**

3.

Understand overarching business and project objectives

What are the overall strategic objectives of the organisation? What challenges is the organisation facing? What are the specific channel shift targets set by the leadership, and how do they link to the business goals?

If you haven't already, you need to understand and set Key Performance Indicators (KPIs) for the project. These will state the project's guiding principles too, so should be referred back to throughout planning and delivery.

Anything that doesn't contribute to these goals should be challenged appropriately.

4.

Planning for iterative development

This is all about planning to launch a Minimum Viable Product (MVP) or launchpad solution that meets essential criteria needed to deliver a working solution quickly and then planning new functionality releases after launch.

It's not about launching with the perfect solution on day one then sitting back.

Why do this?

- ◔ **You get a solution up and running faster**
- ◔ **You don't waste time building non-essential functionality that might not get used**
- ◔ **You can use real user data from a live system to inform further development**

1. **Set the vision for the ideal end-product.** Based on the research from the stakeholder and customer workshops, understanding of the current offering, personas and organisational aims – what is the ultimate, gold-standard system we're looking to build?

2. **Strip this vision back to the most essential functionality.** What are the functions needed to meet the essential criteria and what can we get away without? Use this to build a functional specification for your MVP that describes what the system should do and then break this up into manageable chunks to help with allocating out work to the project teams.

3. **Create a backlog for future iterations.** All the non-essential stuff goes here – plus any new ideas you have during delivery. This allows you to focus on delivering what's needed, then prioritise the extra stuff later.

5.

Understand the current offering

If the project is replacing or enhancing an existing system, you need to understand:

- **Functionality – what can it do? What can't it do?**
- **Use of data – who's using it? How often? And how successfully?**
- **User feedback – what do existing users think of it?**

Getting an understanding of this will give you an idea of:

- **What you're *replacing* because it's an essential part of the system**
- **What you're *not replacing* because it isn't being used**
- **What you need to *improve* because it isn't working**
- **What you can *enhance* because it isn't working hard enough**

This provides us with a basis for a Minimum Viable Product (MVP) or Launchpad offering. In other words – what's the minimum amount we need to do to replace the current system?

You will also be able to see quite quickly where we can make some quick wins with the MVP. The most obvious area for a customer-facing digital platform like a self-service portal would be the user interface – replacing that with a better, easier to use version will enhance every aspect of the system, giving the perception that big changes have been made, even if functionality is essentially the same.

You will also get a view of where the new system can be enhanced against the system it's replacing, either as part of an MVP or in a future iteration.

If you are introducing a brand new system like a new self-service portal then it's helpful to know:

- **What other organisations that have implemented similar systems have done – what went well and what didn't go so well?**
- **What do *you want* users to be able to do with the system? Where can the organisation benefit from this system through greater automation?**

Again, this information helps to establish the minimum specification for a viable launch. Notice that the last list didn't include asking customers what they want? This will come later!

Building customer personas

Building customer personas is an extremely helpful exercise for a customer-facing digital project. It enables you to create, in broad brush strokes, a view of the customer groups you're looking to service as an organisation.

Typically, up to six persona groups should cover all audiences. The information needed to construct each group includes:

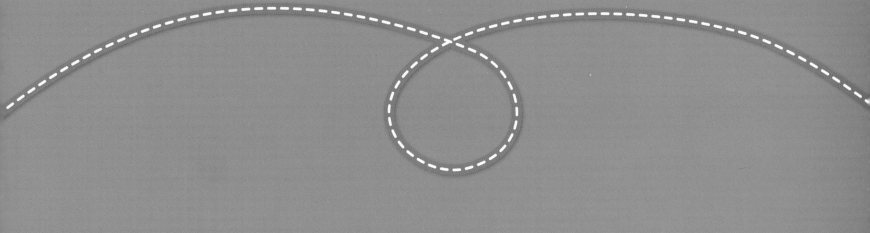

Chapter Five

- **Age group / gender bias if appropriate**
- **Their pain points – what are the main problems they are trying to solve?**
- **Primary and secondary needs – what do they want to do?**
- **Context of use – what devices do they use? How do they typically interact with us?**
- **Your goals for this group – what would be a good outcome for your organisation? What kind of customer do you want them to be? Who in the business has goals for this group?**

Once created, these groups can be prioritised. This can be a difficult exercise, as the temptation is to rank everyone as important. Creating a scoring matrix by giving each persona a score out of five in the following areas can help:

- **Percentage of audience** – The proportion of your customer base this group represents
- **Importance** – The importance of this group to your organisation based on your objectives
- **Potential to satisfy online** – The ease of satisfying this group's needs online
- **Potential impact on internal workload** – The amount of work this group would take to service offline
- **£ lifetime value** – Financial value to the organisation over the customer's lifetime if this workload was taken online

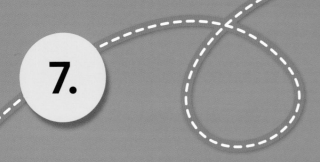

7.

Conducting customer & stakeholder interviews

Stakeholder engagement

It's critical to engage with customer-facing stakeholders within the business when building a customer-facing platform.

- **What are the most common queries these colleagues are asked by customers?**
- **What are the biggest frustrations for them when it comes to doing their job?**

This will often reveal areas that could be automated for the benefit of staff and customer alike. This might be because the information that customers are after is the same regardless who is asking, or because the answer follows a logical and defined path. Repairs or rent payments are a classic example.

Customer engagement

The most successful projects always start with engaging with customers and continue to do so right the way through to planning, taking part in programme management sessions and testing.

The key with customer engagement is to ask the right questions. It's worth delving into replies to questionnaires to discover more. For example, many residents have reported that they 'don't use the internet,' but upon further inquiry, they do shop online, use Facebook and watch movies on Netflix. Many people are more digital-ready than they themselves realise.

At this stage, you are not asking customers to tell you what the solution is, you're asking them to tell you what the problems are so you can decide how to solve them. Obviously this will involve discussing your current offering but it might also involve talking about other platforms they use and what they like about them. This dimension will be discussed further in the next chapter.

8.

Understand the IT Landscape

The functional specification will identify what the system needs to do, the technical part identifies *how* the system will do what it needs to do.

Part of that will involve integrating with other systems like a Housing Management system, Dynamic Repairs Scheduler, contact centre software, smart energy systems, social media, bots and more. You would typically look to understand:

- **What are the current systems and versions being used?**
- **What new systems do you have and how do you assess what is needed from them?**
- **What documentation do you have on those systems?**
- **Do you have documented APIs / Web Services? Who's your contact there? What's the relationship like?**
- **Is there an SLA / agreement / contract?**
- **What are the future plans for these systems? Planned / imminent upgrades? Replacement?**

Once you understand this, you can build a technical specification which describes how the system will work. We recommend, where possible, to build a proof of concept to ensure connections between systems are robust.

Compromises may be needed here too based on limitations of the systems being integrated with so this needs to be factored into the plan.

9.

Next step: delivery

With a primed organisational mindset, a forensic analysis of existing communications channels, an understanding of the IT infrastructure, a coherent plan for automation, a single accurate database, and a roadmap for digital transformation and a team accountable for delivering it, you are all set for delivery.

Key Elements of a Strong Plan

- Inquire deeply into current communications patterns, to create a matrix that informs what can and should be automated.

- Set ambitious deadlines, and hold people accountable to them.

- Set out a clear roadmap, with an understanding of how it can be navigated.

- Be flexible, but in response to genuinely unexpected problems, or feedback from customers – not as a way of endlessly deferring deadlines.

- Incorporate the customer's view from the planning stage; ultimately the purpose of channel shift is to enhance their quality of life.

- Understand and prioritise your audience by creating personas that define respective customer groups, and use these to identify quick wins and to inform prioritisation of project areas.

- Establish positive relationships with system vendors and third party suppliers and get clarity on their availability and SLAs - they'll need to work closely with you and possibly even each other to deliver the project.

- Set up a project board made up of key internal stakeholders from across the business to both own and drive the project forward, inform priorities and help communicate progress across the business.

- Map out how and where your IT systems can / need to be incorporated into the project and if technical integrations are needed, establish quickly whether APIs or Web Services exist to facilitate this. If so, what costs (if any) are associated with using them?

- An understanding of the wider IT landscape in your organisation is key too. Are any key systems being replaced imminently in the near future? If so – what's the impact on the project? How easy will it be to swap out any integrations later and avoid delaying progress shorter term?

- Be clear on where compromises can (and might need to) be made, and be prepared to make them. Your ultimate vision may not be achievable in the short term – but you might be able to launch with an improved service and build on it later to reach your ultimate end goal. Prioritisation is the key – this will be discussed further in Chapter 6.

06
Delivery:
Implementing the Shift

In an agile company, implementing channel shift includes a creative and responsive element – it is not just a rigid roll-out of defined tasks to a fixed timetable.

The exact sequencing matters less than ensuring the most important bases are covered. As discussed in earlier chapters, attending to the mindset of staff and customers is essential preparation, but this shouldn't hold up necessary development of the technology; it needs to reach a certain level of reliability before roll-out, in order to be accepted.

There is a structure, and a timetable, to the project; flexibility means responding to feedback and events. In practice, successful projects have a well-organised Implementation Team, including the core disciplines: IT, customer service, marketing, probably HR and someone from the chief executive's office (see Practical Planning, Chapter 5). There is likely to be a Digital Implementation Officer, the project manager. This team is active, responsive and decisive. Its members meet regularly and investigate how well implementation is going; they encourage and welcome feedback from all relevant parties, and they have a decision-making protocol for making significant changes through the project. They nominate named 'digital champions' within each team, to encourage channel shift and help teach people how to use the new technology; if not in a formal way, at least by ensuring that there are enough such individuals in key parts of the business.

Richard Eden, Communications Manager at Southway Housing, says:

"We have a Digital Inclusion Officer, and ICT trainers. The Digital Inclusion Officer is often outward-facing, running courses for people who may need training, providing equipment like laptops, looking into ways people can get access to the internet. We have digital champions; people who are particularly savvy, who can help other people in work with these issues. If staff aren't digitally included or channel shifting, they can't preach it; it's essential. A lot of our contact is face-to-face; having access to digital services can enhance your life and opportunities."

You have the RACI (Responsible, Accountable, Consulted, Informed) chart described in Chapter 5 that outlines team roles during delivery. This now needs to be communicated and acted upon. The project manager should be chasing this up and logging progress. It is helpful to set deadlines and closely monitor them against internal Service Level Agreements with departments and team members, to keep momentum going and stick to these to keep the project on track.

A helpful discipline is to instil the mindset that everyone is responsible for ensuring the project can and does proceed. Our channel shift survey indicates that there is a mixed view as regards confidence in organisational ability to achieve project objectives on time and to budget. There is markedly more confidence at the most senior levels, indicating potential issues with skills and engagement in other parts of the organisation (see Chart 1). This is reinforced by another survey question, showing that 'internal blockers' were the most cited source of frustration (see Chart 2).

Project management tools help keep track of progress, ideas and individual project elements and put your plan into action. Tools like Jira and VSTS (Visual Studio Team Services) can help agile teams break up the project into manageable chunks, assist with allocation of tasks among teams and help track progress against the plan.

This approach helps project owners keep a top-level view when reporting back to the business, and it helps those responsible for delivery get the granular information they need to work. Examples of categorisation of tasks are:

Epic: a high-level requirement or body of work that expresses a business requirement

Feature: a specific solution to a business requirement that sits within an Epic

User Stories: a description of a functional capability that delivers all or part of a feature, described from the point of view of an end-user

Task: work needed to deliver a user story

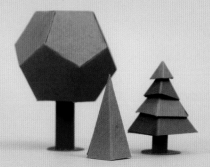

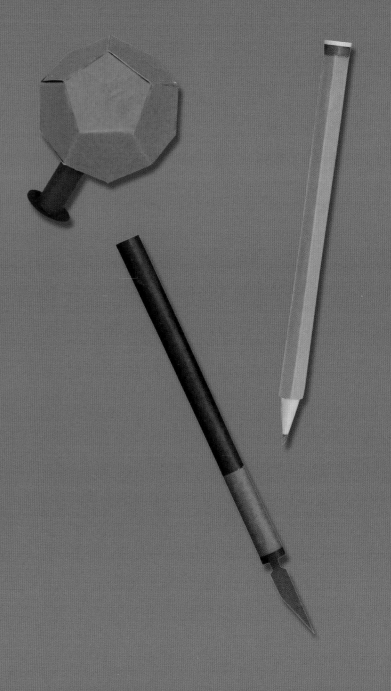

Implementing

What the confidence of delivering to the right channel looks like and the frustration it brings.

Chart 1: Ability to deliver

What is your confidence in your organisation's ability to procure and deliver the right channel shift projects on budget and on time by organisational level?

	Low confidence	Neutral	High confidence
C-Suite/Directors	17%	59%	24%
Heads of Service	44%	28%	28%
Manager	60%	36%	3%
Officers	43%	40%	17%

Channel Shift Survey 2018

Chart 2: Source of frustrations

What are the biggest frustrations during delivery of channel shift projects?

Internal blockers	34%
Working with third-party suppliers	22%
Getting buy-in from customers	18%
Poor communication	13%
I don't know / other	13%

Channel Shift Survey 2018

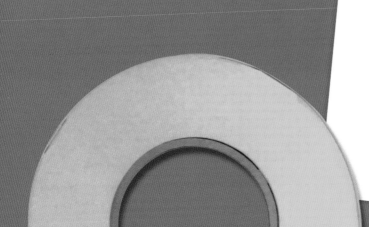

Full integration

Channel shift ultimately involves rethinking and streamlining the whole process involved with delivering a service. There is little or no efficiency saving, or service improvement, where an email simply replaces a letter and simply goes to an inbox for someone to action it when they have time, transferring the request to another system.

With true channel shift, everything is integrated, including with outside contractors such as a maintenance company. So the request goes directly from the mobile device of the customer to that of the service provider, the appointment is agreed and everyone's diary is updated in real time. For this you need a Dynamic Resource Scheduling (DRS) system as part of your technical specification.

Boris Worrall, Chief Executive of Rooftop Housing Group, describes how this process can be challenging and time-consuming. "What you can't do is implement a digital process on an analogue process and be miles better. If you email us to book a repair, you may as well phone us.

"Where things like repairs break down is in the hand-off. Someone phones for a repair, contractors send someone to an address, and they need to arrive at a certain time. There are four or five things that can go wrong. A digital process has to cut through those hand-offs. This is much more difficult and complicated than it sounds. We're working through that."

Matt Cooney, Chief Executive of PA Housing, says: "If you want to change people's behaviour, you have to make sure that the digital channel works, and works well. Where we want to end up is that if someone orders a repair, it goes directly to the engineer's scheduling system, at a date that's convenient for them, and there's a text confirmation, similar to Amazon. Then, when they turn up for the repair, there is tracking so it [the system] can say when they're going to arrive. So it's similar to the retail experience that people have."

Such comparison with a tech giant points to an important consideration as regards who has to take the lead. While engaging the customer from an early stage is helpful, it is important to remain aware of the asymmetry of information. If residents are not aware of the latest systems, and how they can improve service, it would be unfair to expect them to guide the process. This is the duty of those with the technical know-how within the organisation and its partners. The purpose of engagement is to discover the problems in customers' daily lives, and how the housing provider can help solve or alleviate them, using technology where appropriate. If you take a comparison with smartphones, Apple engineers based their invention on their own innovative ideas, using their understanding of what the technology they were developing could do, not on customer research. Customers had not thought of the idea.

For all that full integration and digital channel shift is the goal for many organisations, it is still possible to streamline parts of the process without a fully automated end-to-end solution – for example, enabling

> **"If you want to change people's behaviour, you have to make sure that the digital channel works, and works well."**

> **Matt Cooney**
> PA Housing

ordering of a repair via an iPad and securing an AM or PM slot for the appointment, while work towards full integration with the contractors' scheduling is proceeding. While simply replacing a phone call with an email is inadequate, there are options for partial automation that can bring tangible benefits as you roll out the full solution. It is better to automate some elements well, than go for an over-ambitious modernisation programme where the resources or the project management are inadequate.

A few companies have sought full automation and all the latest technology, such as voice-activated software and augmented reality, all in one go, in order to create headlines, but then have taken on too much. Better to proceed at a pace that is comfortable for the organisation. 'Scope creep' can also occur – that is, people noting a new innovation and wanting to bring it in; this can sometimes be incorporated into a project, but it has to be properly planned and resourced.

A major channel shift can be a two- or three-year project, costing 10% of the organisation's turnover. It is helpful for morale to achieve some straightforward objectives early on – some 'quick wins' – moreover, rapid implementation can help with the piloting and iteration, which are habits of highly innovative companies. A concept that helps is that of the 'Minimum Viable Product', or MVP, which can be brought into use relatively quickly, tested and either rejected or improved (see also Practical Planning Process, Chapter 5).

This underlines the need for a multi-disciplinary approach, involving all key elements of the organisation, so that there is a deep understanding by the Implementation Team of the existing organisational capability, and how it can be strengthened.

We recommend building 12-week reviews into long-term digital transformation plans. The review should include future-gazing, an assessment of new and likely future technological developments, and reports from the ground on implementation, taking into account the customer experience. These reviews ask: What's coming? What's happening? What's changing?

"It is helpful for morale to achieve some straightforward objectives early on – some 'quick wins'"

Technical delivery and dispute resolution

Technical elements of a project delivery can be the most challenging. This involves working with multiple third-party suppliers, who will have their own priorities, challenges and timescales, to get often complex systems talking to each other.

Ultimately though, this exercise is just still a bunch of people working on a solution with a common goal and that's what's so key to remember: however technical the problem is, it's people who will solve it.

Channel Shift Survey 2018

Almost a quarter (22.4%) of our channel shift survey respondents said working with third-party suppliers was their biggest frustration during project delivery.

One of the concerns organisations rightly have when embarking on this element of a channel shift project is, 'what happens when there's a critical problem and supplier A thinks it's supplier B's problem to fix and vice versa?'

This is where a pragmatic and practical viewpoint must be taken. As with any dispute, the best way to resolve is to discuss, person to person and this situation is no different. In our experience, the sooner we can have a conversation directly with responsible parties the sooner

issues and blockers get resolved – this is the case on all project aspects, including technical integrations.

User testing is an extremely helpful discipline. Taking an iterative approach to the project, as described in Chapter 5, you launch with an MVP (Minimum Viable Product), and keep building on that with regular releases. This allows user testing to take place early and often, with the solution being improved at each iteration. This can and should involve both internal stakeholders and customers. This group of beta testers will offer valuable human insight into the project outputs prior to launch, providing an 'outside' perspective. It may even bring ideas that can be carried forward into new features in the future.

An empowered, learning organisation

Transforming the culture, so that the organisation is more of a learning organisation, with greater levels of multi-skilling, helps with channel shift. At Trafford Housing, for example, repair engineers are encouraged to coach customers in how to use online services, so when they turn up, say, to fix the boiler, if the repair hasn't been ordered online, they give a tutorial to the resident on how to do so in future – a very quick and efficient teaching method, compared to arranging a course or digital training day.

Another helpful discipline is to ensure that internal processes for staff are automated – such as booking a meeting room, claiming mileage expenses, and so on. There is still a fair amount of paperwork involved in such procedures in some organisations, so it helps with preparation for customer-facing channel shift, as well as improving internal efficiency, to modernise all staff-related processes also.

At Orbit, digital channel shift has resulted in 96% of tenancy sign-ups being handled online by the tenant, well above the 70% target set by the planners at the outset of the programme in 2015. The remaining 4% are still done online, but with help from a housing officer. **Kevin Hornsby**, Head of Tenancy Sustainment at the association, attributes the success to detailed planning for the switch, which was branded internally as Orbit Move, very high staff engagement, and commitment to making the new channels swifter and easier for clients. The organisation held a total of 100 sessions on Orbit Move for staff and residents; Orbit has won a National Innovation Award, and a Chartered Institute of Housing award for Best use of Technology in the Sector. Another key feature of the system has been an emphasis on expanding service options for residents – for example, in the case of formerly homeless residents, putting them in touch directly with providers of grants for furniture.

One of the key elements of ensuring that take-up is so high has been the emphasis on customer service. The switch to digital has helped a more welcoming approach to new tenants, for example. Before the transformation, an employee would sit down with a new resident and take them through a long, detailed paper contract, clause by clause, "when they just wanted to get the keys," says Kevin.

New media open up options to make implementation programmes participative and fun. Sovereign Housing, for example, used Virtual Reality at a senior leadership conference to talk about digital transformation, as opposed to a conventional talk with Powerpoint slides, "which would be a bit dull," says **Robin Middleton**, Head of Digital Marketing at Sovereign. The result was a virtual reality tour of the House of the Future. He adds: "You're the eyes and the ears as you are walking around the house… You're wearing Google Cardboard on your phone. You can look around the kitchen, look at the boiler. We can hopefully use this to explain to people how these things are going to come about."

Communication

In our channel shift survey, 51.2% felt their organisation communicated progress back to the organisation poorly or not at all during delivery of channel shift projects, while 33.7% said internal blockers were the biggest frustration during project delivery.

This doesn't have to be the case. An internal staff conference is a good opportunity to discuss the project and gain views of staff as well as communicate progress while you have a captive audience. There may be a staff newsletter or intranet where regular company news is shared. Many organisations have either set up or reinvigorated their internal interactive media as part of the preparation of mindset for channel shift (see Chapter 4). These are the perfect forums to keep the organisation enthused, engaged and updated as the project progresses.

These are basic examples – but communications and marketing teams will be key to making this happen and will be able to work on a communications strategy for keeping internal and external stakeholders in the loop. It's up to the project steering group to ensure these teams are involved, and that adequate resource is planned around them.

"The 12-week reviews should ask: What's coming? What's happening? What's changing?"

Data handling and security

It is only natural that customers, and some staff, will want reassurance on data security. The details held by housing associations on residents are very personal, and high-profile data breaches in recent years, including at major international companies, have caused anxiety on this important issue.

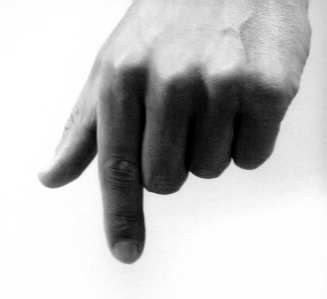

Dan Moraga, Programme Manager for Digital Transformation at PA Housing, says: "The education piece is also about allaying fears around security. If there has been a big breach reported repeatedly through the media, often that can be a turn-off for some of our customer base… We are trying to create services that we are confident that for users will work well and be reliable and accessible; that they like and that work as well as other services they're probably using – like the banks, Amazon and so on."

Boris Worrall, Chief Executive of Rooftop Housing Group, draws attention to another potential niggle with online communication, which is unwanted sales and marketing information. He has encountered little concern over data security, but notes that some customers have been unhappy about receiving marketing material about house sales and so on. The need for self-discipline, for resisting the impulse to overload customers – and staff for that matter – with information is paramount during implementation and afterwards.

Sensitivity and respecting tenants' rights to privacy are important considerations, given greater urgency with the introduction of tighter regulation with the European General Data Protection Regulations, which came into force in May 2018, strengthening all citizens' rights to opt out of databases and of unsolicited messages, and sharply increasing fines for organisations that are in breach. Data security and handling of data generally should be considered at every stage of delivery. Each touchpoint with each platform that handles, hands-off and presents data to an end user should be securely encrypted and only accessible to those who need the information. This is also the case for storage of data – only the data that is needed should be stored within the system and the places where it is stored also need to be secure.

There is a tension between greater data security, and ease of log-in arrangements for customers, issues that we discuss further in Chapter 7, and also in Chapter 8, where we discuss how new technology can improve the options for handling this balance.

No one left behind

An emphasis made throughout our work in this sector, including in the interviews for this book, is that a social housing provider needs to offer choice, and to have, where possible, services tailored to individual needs.

Housing associations will often establish a risk-rating system to identify those who are most vulnerable. In a sensitively and well-handled channel shift, more specialist time from housing officers can be freed up to spend on the cases with the most need – indeed, this is one of the primary aims of the shift in an age of limited resources (see The Housing Officer in Chapter 2).

Having said that, new technology can still quicken and improve services that may superficially appear to be too sensitive for digital channels to be involved. Take anti-social behaviour, for example. While the most serious examples require direct intervention from trained staff – housing officers, or the police in the most serious cases – others can be dealt with differently. Reporting graffiti, for example, can be done by taking a photograph on a smartphone and emailing it to the relevant office, or uploading via a web-based portal or app. This is quicker and cheaper than the resident telephoning a contact centre, and gives more accurate information. This method includes automatic recording of the date, time and exact geographical location, helping both to identify the exact nature of the problem, and to be held as evidence in the most serious cases. In the cases where graffiti includes direct threats and represents a hate crime, the matter will need to be escalated; but having photographic evidence transmitted instantly helps rapid and appropriate intervention in these cases, also.

This example points to the importance of identifying and categorising services and needs in a precise, granular way, rather than relying on headings that are too broad.

Organisational resilience: sticking with it

No project in human history has ever gone without a hitch, without an unexpected event that may be minor, or may threaten to knock the entire programme off course. There will be kit that arrives late or has a technical glitch; a sickness absence of a key team member; serious differences of opinion on project priorities, and so on.

Successful teams cannot avoid or prevent unplanned difficulties, but they have robust ways of dealing with them. This means maintaining lines of communication, close relationship with suppliers, open discussion at your 12-week reviews, and maintaining clarity and lines of accountability with reference to the RACI (Responsible, Accountable, Consulted, Informed) chart – see Chapter 5.

These are features of organisational resilience that successful teams build into their daily ways of working. Projects that are completed on time and under budget, and which overachieve on the targets set, have often featured as many unexpected problems as those that end in crisis. The difference lies in the quality of the project management, and the adaptability and

preparedness of the team. The foundation built by understanding and preparing mindset (see Chapter 4) and building lines of communication and teamwork, really comes into its own when the implementation team faces major challenges, including those of the unexpected kind.

While the planning and implementation of key projects – automation of rent accounts, repairs booking, and so on – comprise major elements of a channel shift, it would be a mistake to think exclusively in terms of finite projects with an end date. The most effective organisations are learning organisations; they monitor, collect feedback, iterate and continuously improve services. The main disciplines of monitoring and measuring are the subject of the next chapter.

Key disciplines for delivery of channel shift

- Ensure the main Digital Implementation Team meets regularly, communicates honestly, and respects the RACI chart

- Keep a calm head when unexpected setbacks occur. It helps to have contingency plans as part of risk assessment and planning

- Try to have some achievable objectives for early on in the project; some quick wins to boost morale, and from which to learn about implementation

- Hold 12-weekly reviews. These should include an element that is outward-facing and looking at possible future technological developments, as well as reviewing progress internally

- Build a learning organisation; remember to automate internal processes where possible, as well as customer services where appropriate. Teach all staff to become digital enablers

07
Measurement and Improvement:
Monitoring the impact

Continual monitoring of the impact of channel shift on the customers, and the organisation, is an essential discipline. It will come naturally to the project teams that have spent time preparing the mindset, empowering digital champions and with clear goals based on improving quality of life for customers.

The point of measurement is not simply a 'pass or fail' test as to whether take-up is high; monitoring, or measuring, is more the discipline of continuous inquiry of the agile organisation. It's a means to an end, with the purpose being ongoing improvement to service. It involves delving into the reasons behind the popularity or otherwise of a new communications channel, and inquiring into related features, and the quality of service. For example, is low take-up caused by weaknesses in training residents on the technology, poor user interface on mobile devices, or a combination? Only through continual monitoring, analysis of patterns of communication, and qualitative inquiry into the customer experience, can you answer these telling questions.

In both these dimensions of monitoring and analysis, quantitative and qualitative, there's a need for depth. In the case of quantitative analysis, not just to look at uptake of a new channel, but to look at the patterns overall – whether new media are replacing old media, or whether there is duplication. In the case of checking service levels and the customer experience, this inquiry needs to assess quality of life, not just a superficial satisfaction score. While the two areas of analysis – patterns of communication and the reasons for them – are separate, the deepest understanding comes from considering them together, and linking this to key business indicators.

A matrix used at the outset of channel shift to identify pre-existing patterns (see Sovereign Housing example, Chapter 5), can be used again during implementation and after, to identify the trends, using multiple indicators and interpreting the many signals. For example, if online communication has increased but calls haven't fallen, this may look like a failure in a narrow framing of the issue of channel shift. If, however, tenants are happier and rent arrears are decreasing, some important trends, including for the business, are positive. This indicates a sensitive approach is most appropriate, encouraging further use of online methods, rather than simply cutting back on the telephone service.

Dan Moraga, Housing Project Manager at PA Housing, says: "It's an approach of continuous improvement, monitoring feedback from users. This has enabled us to zero in on the parts that are working really well, and also showed us what wasn't working – eg, no one's clicked; or they've clicked but we never saw a case resulting. It's a constant feedback loop going on. This is less effort than getting groups of customers to come in in office hours to discuss a certain path or process.

"We measure performance in many ways. We collect hard numbers, such as how many people are logging on; intelligence on what are the most popular processes. Then we take all of that and try to compare to call data. For example, payments: we take about 2,500 payments online, then we look at the total number of payments, the trends – increasing, decreasing? – always using it to look at how the channel is really working."

While results from quantitative and qualitative information are best analysed together, the data-gathering processes are quite different. We summarise some of the most important methods in the sections that follow.

Quantitative methods

Tracking tools, such as Google Analytics, HotJar and others, enable you to securely and non-invasively track web-based platforms as they are used by customers.

These tools can provide data-driven insight into the performance of the platform, based on the way in which users are interacting with it. In doing so, this can help pinpoint areas where there may be issues requiring further investigation and improvement or optimisation.

These types of reporting can provide, among other types of information:

Click-maps or heat-maps that show where users are clicking on a page.

Scroll depth maps that show how far users are venturing down a page.

Goal tracking – to track completion and abandonment of specific conversion points involving a pre-set series of actions, such as forms being completed or successful / failed logins.

Event tracking to ascertain when and how often specific events occur – these might be clicking specific buttons, for instance.

Search tracking to monitor the terms entered into a search function, where one exists.

Traffic tracking to show which pages are being visited, or not visited, for how long and from which devices.

Adding a quick and quantitatively measurable feedback mechanism within your platform can also help. With this, when a user completes a process or is served information after a query, the system checks if that information solved the problem by asking a Yes / No question, or reviews how useful the information was by requesting a star rating. The benefits of this are:

- For the customer: this rating information can be aggregated and made public, so others can see the average rating or number of users who said this solved their problem – lending authority and trust to the content or process.

- For the organisation: quantitative data shows how helpful the information that they're providing is, and how and where processes need to be improved.

Net Promoter Score (NPS) is another quantitative tool that many organisations use to measure customer satisfaction and loyalty. It's predicated on asking a single question:

How likely is it that you would recommend our company/product/service to a friend or colleague?

Qualitative methods

Qualitative analysis is not 'softer' than quantitative information, and is of equal importance in monitoring and measuring the effectiveness of channel shift, helping you to understand the reasons that underlie different patterns of communication. Conventional methods such as survey questions play a role and, increasingly, technology can help with the analysis. A few techniques that have been proven to be useful...

Benchmarking against other organisations can help set reasonable targets and aspirations. How are other organisations performing against their objectives? How have they achieved those results? What do their customers think? How do you compare to all of this?

Customer satisfaction surveys – Running regular satisfaction surveys is something many housing organisations already do, but it's important to ensure you ask the right questions to give you useful insight.

Sentiment tracking – It's helpful to look at overall sentiment from customers by analysing the information coming through on existing channels. Some call centre software enables you to pull out phrases and words that are used and allocate sentiment to them. Equally, software can be used to analyse data sent digitally via website forms and email to ascertain the tone of communications from customers.

Beta testing – Getting users to test an actual working product is an effective way of seeing how well new platform developments perform in a live environment before they are finalised.

Eye tracking – This is where we ask a user to complete a series of tasks on a platform while wearing a pair of glasses that track where they are looking on the page while completing their task. This data is overlaid onto a recording of their session and complemented with a short interview where they are interviewed about their experience.

When it comes to assessing the customer experience, **Claire Bayliss**, consultant with 3C Consultants, highlights the weakness of superficial satisfaction scores. You need to dig deeper, she says, citing one example she was involved in where the service provider was registering 90% satisfaction, yet managers were aware that parts of the system were not working well.

"So they went out and got a detailed customer service report and it came out at 65%," she says. "It was a shock to them; yet it is difficult to measure satisfaction. They had tried to simplify it too much [in their internal survey], make it quick and simple, just a couple of ticks.

They were missing that a lot of customers were happy with the front-line staff, but felt let down by policies and procedures. So they had been asked: 'Were the staff polite, pleasant?' and so on, and of course they were, but what you wanted was answers to questions like: 'Did this intervention resolve your situation?'"

For example, on repairs, it's worth looking at trends over time, informed by exception reporting. If there is a surge in repairs, you need to know why. If the online service is not meeting expectations, this could be problems with the portal, or with the maintenance service, or both.

Qualitative and quantitative measures highlight problems and issues to be addressed in the current forms of communication and service delivery within a housing provider. Technology can now help you go further, with predictive measurement, which can help you identify emerging and potential issues.

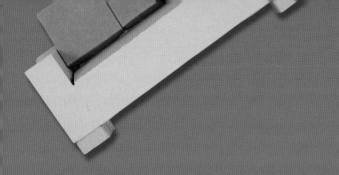

Predictive Measurement

Within the home, smart appliances and devices can automatically highlight when parts are weakening or may need replacing.

Smart boilers are a good example – with many able to identify problems before they occur, enabling an engineer to come out and fix it before an issue arises. Such preventative measures can be cheaper than repair and, of course, there is no interruption of supply. It reduces stress for the tenant, by taking the onus away from them to report the issue.

Predictive technology is not only for appliances, but can also help identify people-related issues. Some Artificial Intelligence (AI)-based tracking tools enable you to monitor user activity within a self-service portal that can highlight to housing officers an emerging issue of concern. For instance:

- Marie has been a tenant for the previous six years and she's a single parent with two young children.

- She generally pays her rent on time and in full every week, but recently she's moved to Universal Credit and she's now starting to pay rent late.

- Marie's late payments are picked up and she's served a link to an interactive budget calculator.

- With the help of this service, she manages to pay on time the next week, but she quickly starts slipping back to late payments, and begins to go into arrears.

- Marie receives some more content on household budget planning and debt advice over the next couple of weeks. This includes information on alternative payment options offered by the self-service portal.

- The situation begins to improve when Marie sets up a recurring rent payment via her self-service portal. This means her rent is now paid automatically every week – but she's still in arrears for previously missed payments.

- This prompts a call from Angela at the call centre, who helps Marie come up with an arrangement plan to clear her rent arrears.

- Marie clears her rent arrears within six weeks thanks to the plan and, thanks to her recurring rent payment, no longer needs to worry about missing a payment.

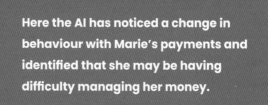

Here the AI has noticed a change in behaviour with Marie's payments and identified that she may be having difficulty managing her money.

KPI Measurement

Just as important as the ability to measure user behaviour and satisfaction quantitatively and qualitatively, is ensuring you use this data to report on the right things. Key Performance Indicators (KPIs) should be set as early as possible in the process, as discussed in previous chapters. They need to be linked to overall organisational objectives, but equally must be appropriate to the platform being measured.

For a self-service platform aimed at helping achieve channel shift, for instance, **adoption** and **advocacy** are useful criteria to consider as a way to measure channel shift.

Adoption is an indicator that customers are using the platform. So this could be measured by number of registrations, subsequent logins and/or use of specific features and functions.

Advocacy is where customers are actively using the platform as a channel of choice. This is a little harder to measure and requires a mix of data. Here you would need to contrast call centre data with portal tracking data, and use Net Promoter Score (NPS) to get a measure of loyalty and customer satisfaction surveys to get a sense of customer sentiment.

Security and Logging In

One issue that can emerge at the measurement and monitoring phase is that take-up is hindered by problems some individuals have with the logging-in procedure. Not all customers are comfortable with IDs, reference numbers and passwords, nor efficient at remembering them or keeping them safe.

This requires sensitivity on the part of service providers. **Matt Cooney**, Chief Operating Officer at PA Housing, reports that the security mechanism the association uses is a payment reference number, which is issued in order to register for the app. To log in, the resident needs to know the number, and add some personal data.

He says: "There is a high abandon rate, when applying the number. People just haven't got that number to hand. If they ring up, we can send to an email address, but they're not doing that. So we're scratching our heads on that." Managers have considered using the NI number, but this is potentially less secure as it will be held on many other databases, including for Universal Credit. "These are issues we have investigated."

This is a long-running issue that systems designers have been grappling with. Some organisations include simple solutions like tooltips on their registration forms that show people, through text and images, exactly where they can find these reference numbers. Another technique is to use a screenshot of a customer letter, with the number circled to show precisely where it can be found.

Promising new technology may be able to offer further help. Some systems can amalgamate data from multiple central databases such as the electoral roll, credit reference agencies, and so on, to verify identification by asking questions that only that person would know, such as: which of these addresses means something to you? It is also possible that biometrics will have a significant role, as we will discuss further in Chapter 8, which covers future developments.

Face-to-face meetings

While the analysis of data, and use of questionnaires and the like do the bulk of the monitoring work, there is still a place for face-to-face communication to supplement this, giving the opportunity for more nuanced communication, or in-depth insight into the customer experience.

Steve Dungworth, Director of Digital Transformation at Accent Housing, says: "We completed a three-day review of the repairs process, from reporting to completion: involved a lot of internal stakeholders, and also included a customer, for the whole three-day workshop. Their insight was invaluable. They were made to feel welcome; they pointed out the obvious, as in: We don't necessarily need a repair completed quickly, but we like it when you turn up when you say you will."

The discipline of improvement, monitoring and iteration is continual, he says. "It is like painting the Forth Road Bridge, looking at the next improvement, website functionality: being accessible to your own staff as customers, help them understand from the customer's perspective."

At the time of interview, Accent had set itself the aim of going completely paperless within five to ten years, with work having begun on an electronic documentation management project for the second phase of its channel shift project, to remove 44 different forms. Managers had also started talks with suppliers about Artificial Intelligence, in the area of predictive

questions, with the aim of embedding in the website chatbots that can help customers directly. "We have worked out, from online records, that there are only 40 questions that customers ask us," says Steve.

Chatbot systems have to be highly sophisticated to ensure that replies are tailored to the situation; while there may be only 40 questions, there will be many different ways of asking them. There may still need to be the option of speaking to a call centre adviser in exceptional circumstances. This technology is developing rapidly, however, and it is likely that the offerings will have enhanced sensitivity and sophistication in the coming few years. We will discuss emerging technologies more in Chapter 8.

Analytics tools can yield information on where people are on a website, what they are clicking for information, and so on. **Rich Harvey**, Head of IT Housing Solutions at the association, says: "That information will help us. A lot of people are looking, clicking all over the place, once that feedback will speak to different users to say: it used to take this long; would this be a better way of finding the information? We are working with the customer engagement team on this."

Early indications were that significant numbers had switched to online channels for managing their rent account, but uptake was slower for repairs, so the team had begun looking at why. On the positive side, those requesting repairs were mostly doing so out of hours, and in total some 75% of self-service webchats were out of hours, so the switch away from a 'nine-to-five' mindset was well under way.

> ## "We have worked out, from online records, that there are only 40 questions that customers ask us"
>
> **Steve Dungworth**
> Accent Housing

Demographics of those adapting readily to online channels are worth studying. What you often find is that, while the common perception is that older generations are less digitally savvy, there is huge variation within older age groups. "Actually, they're one of the most active in trying to learn this new world," says **Richard Eden**, Communications Manager at Southway Housing. "They attend the classes; know from friends and family, or take it on themselves. I think we've learned a lot more about where the issues come from, or blockages with regards to access. It can be a surprise; not the demographics you expect."

Another surprise for many with follow-up and monitoring exercises has been the widespread use of mobile devices, including among many older people. There are around 42 million smartphone users in the UK. The proportion of the population with a smartphone rose from 17% to 78% between 2008 and 2018, according to the telecoms regulator Ofcom's 2018 Communications Market Report. It also found that one-fifth of British adults were spending more than 40 hours each week on their phone, with 64% of adults regarding it as an essential part of their lives. While younger people were heavier users, there's a distribution curve within each demographic, and some older citizens were very active. The average time online per day was 3.5 to 4 hours for the 18-24 age group; it was lower for those aged over 55, but higher than you might think, at around 2 hours. [1]

The sharply rising use of smartphones means that housing providers need to ensure that their self-service portals are well suited for mobile and tablet devices, in some cases making design alterations in the light

of early feedback during a channel shift programme. PA Housing found during its monitoring that a full 70% of online access to the association's services by residents was from a mobile device, rather than a PC. "One of our assumptions would have been the opposite," says **Dan Moraga**, Housing Project Officer. "We can make assumptions about the sector that are shown to be false."

PA Housing underwent redesigns to ensure the online service was more mobile friendly. It also offers a wide range of services via mobile devices, including the ability to post pictures and report issues with the communal area.

The association has also found that, with channel shift, they are communicating with a wider, more diverse range of customers. When contact was mostly through face-to-face meetings: "...you tended to see the same people all the time," says Dan.

"The point of measurement is not a simple 'pass or fail' test; it's continuous inquiry"

[1] Communications Market Report 2018, Ofcom, 2 August 2018, https://www.ofcom.org.uk/research-and-data/multi-sector-research/cmr

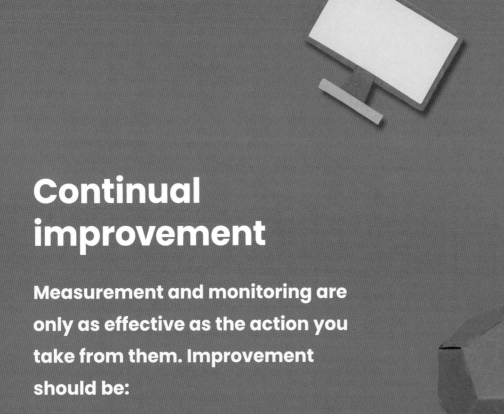

Continual improvement

Measurement and monitoring are only as effective as the action you take from them. Improvement should be:

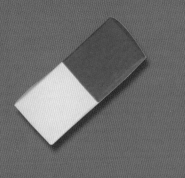

Ongoing

Improvement is not something that should stop – don't allow platforms to stagnate. What was a perfect solution at launch may be outdated in six months' time, or may not be received positively by users.

Agile

Build and release improvements with reference to the roadmap, but with flexibility to address more pressing issues that come up from user testing and monitoring.

Rapid

Produce regular iterations and releases (fortnightly or monthly) that deliver small to medium, incremental improvements.

45% of housing association employees felt that their organisations did little to no work to measure and continually improve customer-facing digital platforms

Our own survey into channel shift found that some housing associations have much scope for making further progress. Nearly half (45.4%) of housing association staff felt that their organisations did little to no work to measure and improve customer-facing digital platforms, while a similar proportion (47.8%) felt that there was little effort to promote and grow the user base of customer-facing digital platforms. For all the

progress that has been made in recent years, these statistics are sobering.

There is a certain symmetry to effective channel shift projects in that they begin and end with analysis and data – indeed, this is an ongoing discipline: inquiring into the real patterns of communication in the business, and their effectiveness. Common narratives, such

48% felt their organisation did little to no work to promote and grow the user-base of its customer-facing digital platforms

as 'People hate change,' or 'Older residents aren't online,' always need regular checking against hard facts, and updating. A heartening development from the implementation and monitoring of channel shift projects has been the revelation that residents who tended not to attend meetings or call on the phone have been brought more into contact with housing association staff, and in some cases, with each other

In Chapter 1, we emphasised that modernising communications technology is not only consistent with the long-established ethos of housing associations; it can be a key way of fulfilling some of their most important aims: creating safe, dignified living spaces, and reducing social isolation.

Key Disciplines When Monitoring Channel Shift

- Look at patterns overall in communication, not just a linear 'phone-to-web' channel shift

- Look at the underlying reasons for preferences in communications channels, and check for duplication and service effectiveness

- A mix of data and qualitative information, analysed together, gives the fullest and most useful intelligence

- Compare the findings of your inquiry against common narratives in the business; use them to challenge the mindset if it is not accurate

- Seek to assess quality of life and customer satisfaction as well as use of media and efficiency savings

08
Concluding Thoughts:
Looking to the future

At the end of a major channel shift project, it's worth looking back at the implementation, and forward at future technologies and the potential they hold.

As noted in Chapter 7, there will have been problems, including unexpected ones, but many of the benefits in terms of service improvements and organisational efficiency can be enjoyed along the way. Celebrating these, while acknowledging the challenges that remain, is helpful. It is not a new observation, but one worth remembering: making mistakes can be a lesson. Something went wrong; but what did we learn? The agile, learning organisation is always looking for ways to improve, and innovation is never a perfect science with perfect implementation. Learning and recovering from things that didn't work out is how the agile business also becomes resilient.

Underlining the need for both agility and resilience is the fact that technology is advancing rapidly – and we summarise some appropriate and thought-provoking developments in this chapter.

People often express regret that they did not begin the *Shift* sooner, to realise the benefits it can bring. Such conscientiousness is admirable, but it is important also to retain a positive outlook, and acknowledge the progress achieved.

Many in the housing space have made huge strides in recent years. And if you feel you are 'not there yet,' then as long as you have a clear, practical vision for the *Shift*, a shared understanding of where you need to get to, then you're on the journey, and moving in the right direction.

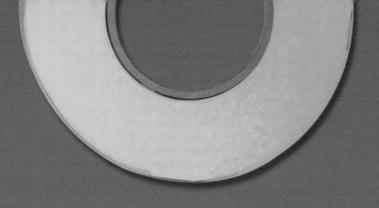

Learning Points

A brief summary of some of the main learning points from the phases of implementation...

Phase 1 Mindset

- Don't make assumptions around people's readiness for channel shift.
- Gather data and conduct surveys. Don't rely on guesswork.
- Make sure the business's leaders are living the cultural change, by being digitally connected, open and communicative.

Phase 2 Planning

- Inquire deeply into current communications patterns to create a matrix that informs what can and should be automated.
- Set out a clear roadmap, with an understanding of how it can be navigated.
- Build in scope for flexibility, so you'll be able to respond to issues.

Phase 3 Delivery

- Try to have some achievable early objectives; some 'quick wins' to boost morale.
- Implement, review and iterate continually, rather than wait for the 'perfect' solution.
- Hold 12-weekly reviews, with a broad agenda and open discussion.

Phase 4 Measurement and Improvement

- Look at patterns overall in communication, not just a linear 'phone-to-web' channel shift.
- Look at the underlying reasons for preferences in communications channels.
- Seek to assess quality of life and customer satisfaction as well use of media and efficiency savings.

Future technology and the latest research

In terms of new and upcoming technology, and how it will expand choice and alter organisational ways of working, we are sometimes asked what will be dominant in 5-10 years' time.

Realistically, that's too far ahead to be able to give a useable forecast. Technology is developing so rapidly that the 18-month to two-year horizon is challenging enough. There are significant breakthroughs in certain areas that are imminent, but whether they reach the tipping point of widespread adoption next month, next year or the year after, is impossible to anticipate with precision. Furthermore, some inventions that are scarcely known today may have a big impact. Going back 15 years, very few people anticipated the invention of the smartphone; now it is the dominant manner of accessing online services.

The possibility of new or imminent disruptive technology shouldn't dissuade you from making some bold investments, however. It is easier to adapt and build onto a modern infrastructure than an ageing one. A useful discipline is to have at least one person attending your 12-weekly review meetings, part of whose role is to monitor and study current and likely future technological developments. The ever-changing nature of technology underlines the importance of building flexibility into the project plans.

Below we summarise the state of play and likely next developments in some of the technological areas most relevant to housing, and discuss some of the possible uses and implications. We also briefly consider the latest anthropological research and findings from neuroscience on the features of healthy communities.

Artificial Intelligence (AI)

AI, also known as machine intelligence, is the simulation of human intelligence by a computer system. Typically, an AI machine is capable of learning, reasoning, and self-correction. The latest machines can effectively learn their own way of problem-solving; they can train themselves.

Virtual assistants like Alexa and Google Assistant are already in use in many homes. At Google's annual developer conference in 2018, the firm unveiled Google Duplex. The company demonstrated the assistant calling a hair salon and booking an appointment on behalf of her 'client'. The AI had a conversation with the salon receptionist, including 'hmms' and 'ers', like a real person, without the individual at the salon realising they were on the phone to a machine.

A **chatbot** is a particular type of AI. It provides an automated, conversational customer inquiry service via either voice or text. Chatbot technology is probably, in the year 2018, at about the stage that apps were seven years earlier, and development could be of particular significance for the housing sector. As discussed in Chapter 7, it is a tricky technology to get right, as there are many different ways of asking the same question; conversely, two similar-sounding questions may be significantly different. As this technology improves in sophistication, it holds the potential to replace the telephone for many inquiries. Chatbots may be lacking in empathy compared with a human being, but they respond immediately and are available out of office hours.

Virtual assistants and chatbots could help supplement call centres in the housing space. Basic out-of-hours phone support is an obvious choice, but a technology like this could be an effective gatekeeper – capable of dealing with less nuanced and sensitive issues, and able to hand off to a human colleague if the caller has a more complex need.

Frameworks like Microsoft's Computer Vision API enable automatic analysis and interpretation of images by AI. The potential applications in the housing space are numerous. For repairs, tools will be built that enable a resident to take a photo of the issue and the AI will read the image, diagnose the issue and arrange for the appropriate fix.

This type of image-recognition technology is already in use now, in a more basic form. Amazon uses Optical Character Recognition (OCR) to facilitate faster payments via its app. The tool allows you to take a photo of your payment card and the software reads the numbers and expiry dates and automatically enters them for you. AI-based software, coupled with hardware sensors on appliances and home equipment like boilers, can already be used to identify and even predict faults or failures before an issue presents itself. This technology has the potential to enable housing providers to proactively manage their stock without having to attend appointments at the home.

Voice technology

Voice technology is rapidly becoming mainstream, through Amazon's popular Alexa tool and others. There could be significant benefits for the social housing sector.

Once installed, a resident can simply ask the device to pay rent, or order a repair. The potential to help people with certain kinds of disabilities is considerable.

Biometrics

Biometrics, of course, is not new. It has been used for many years in high-security places, and more recently by the general population – for example using a fingerprint or facial recognition to unlock a smartphone.

Biometrics is one of the means by which the administrative challenges of personal security and registration and login procedures, discussed in earlier chapters, can be alleviated. To register, a user simply takes a photo of their driver's licence or passport via the platform and takes a short selfie video of themselves. The two are then biometrically compared against each other to establish if this is the same person, and the documents are cross-checked against central third-party sources to establish if they are genuine.

Augmented Reality (AR)

This is a technology that overlays computer-generated images onto a user's view of the real world.

Most typically, AR experiences are delivered via smartphones, with users utilising the device's camera to provide the view of the real world, while the AR software running on the device provides the overlay. At the time of writing, Apple's ARKit2 is the leader in this area – and virtually all current Apple mobile devices are capable of delivering some kind of AR experience, thanks to the built-in capability shipped with their iOS mobile operating system. Current applications of AR include games where the characters and gameplay appear to come to life in your own environment. There are practical applications, too – apps that allow users to measure real-world objects with a virtual tape measure, an AR menu that lets you see dishes on a plate in front of you before you order at a restaurant, and many more.

Coupled with AI-based image recognition technology, AR could be used by housing associations to facilitate repairs and diagnosis, and be a platform for delivering immersive self-help information. For repairs that tenants need to complete themselves, AR could be used to overlay a practical demonstration of how to make the fix onto a real-world environment. For repairs reporting, the user could hold up their device in the area of the repair and tap to highlight the exact location of the problem on the screen.

Virtual Reality

Virtual Reality (VR) is a more immersive experience than AR, but requires additional equipment. This includes headsets and can involve hand-held devices, gloves, harnesses and omnidirectional treadmills.

VR could be used in the housing association of the future to provide property tours delivered by a virtual assistant, itself driven by AI. This could be done to preview developments before they are built and help to sell more units off-plan, but also for general needs: getting potential tenants to see a property without having to visit it. It has already been used by Sovereign Housing Association at an internal presentation to showcase the 'Home of the Future', deploying the Google Cardboard technology (see Chapter 6).

Blockchain technology

A blockchain is computer code used to create a decentralised, permanent, public ledger of value exchanges such as financial payments or asset transfers. Non-blockchain technology tends to rely on a central, private server to hold data but in a blockchain, the ledger is shared between everyone who is using it, rather than being controlled by a central authority. That is what is meant by decentralised and distributed. Transaction records within a blockchain are secured through encryption and each transaction is linked to the next, meaning that, by design, the ledger cannot be edited – only added to.

Smart contracts can be used within a blockchain. These are contracts that automatically transfer money or assets between parties based on the agreed terms. This is opposed to a traditional contract, which relies on the goodwill and diligence of the involved parties to be enforced.

Blockchain as a technological choice is best when you can answer yes to the following:

1. Is it a repeatable process that would benefit from automation?

2. Is it an ongoing transaction process?

3. Are multiple stakeholders taking part?

4. Does one of those stakeholders facilitate the transaction?

5. Is there a specific value: money, data, rights, privileges, being transacted?

6. Is there a requirement for a permanent, unaltered record of these transactions?

If 'yes' is the answer to most of these questions, it's worth considering blockchain.

In housing, blockchain could be used for rental payments, home sales or even lettings. A blockchain, used across the housing sector, with smart contracts enforcing payment of rent between tenants and landlords, could help reduce arrears. It could also make it easier for missed payments to be recovered – even if a tenant were to move between housing organisations. For home sales, this technology could assist in the transfer of funds between parties, as well as deeds of ownership, and other documents linked to the sale.

Human connections

As we have emphasised throughout this book, the ultimate purpose of a housing association is to provide affordable, high-quality accommodation and safe, healthy communities. At its core, the housing sector is about people and their quality of life. For all the talk of technology and its ability to automate manual processes, interpret, act upon and process information and data, it's important for us to remember that.

Scientific research is by no means confined to technology, and there are some valuable recent discoveries in the realms of neuroscience and anthropology that can help us develop strong communities, and help us decide the best role for devices and communications channels. There have been many studies that demonstrate how human beings 'catch' feelings from each other; that moods are contagious. The explanation lies in the 'open loop' nature of the brain's limbic system, our emotional centre: it relies on external stimuli. This explains why the presence of a loved one for someone in intensive care will lower the patient's blood pressure.

In a similar way, in work teams, and in neighbourhoods, healthy emotional connections – friendliness, kindness, effective leadership and so on – will create stronger and happier communities. These findings also underline the importance for housing associations of attending to culture, mindset and employee engagement, as discussed in earlier chapters.

Channel shift means reserving human-to-human contact for the interactions that are of most benefit – for example, a housing officer providing comfort to someone who is lonely and scared; and removing it where it adds no value – sitting with a new tenant to go through a long, tedious paper tenancy agreement, for example.

It doesn't mean ending the personal contact, as many of our interviewees have pointed out. The purpose of new technologies is ultimately to help bond communities, create more supported households, with happier individuals and more sustainable tenancies. For housing providers, a happier workforce and neighbourhood means fewer tenancy breakdowns, rent arrears and problems with anti-social behaviour.

What I Would Have Done Differently

"I would have started the marketing effort earlier. Our approach was: build first, market second. We might have started that earlier, in terms of the numbers of people"

Dan Moraga
Housing Project Manager
PA Housing

"Do it quicker. Why didn't we do it before? We are looking towards integration... You could have integrated asset information. It's very much a one-way module [at the moment]; the online system feeds the housing management system, but it doesn't feed back. That's something we are looking at"

Kevin Hornsby
Head of Tenancy Sustainment
Orbit Housing

"I would be bolder! You can tend to get bogged down in the complexities and risks"

Steve Dungworth
Director of Digital Transformation
Accent Housing

"Probably when we launched the website, we could have switched off some of the offline stuff earlier on, and gone to online only. [But] we wanted more information on how the website works; we didn't want to push people online only for it not to work"

Rich Harvey
Head of IT
Housing Solutions

"I think we should have been really clear about the problems we're trying to fix, not seeing digital as a panacea. If we had spent more time with that definition, rather than lots of digitising, we would be further forward"

Paul Taylor
Innovation Coach
Bromford Housing

"We didn't involve customers enough in the first wave, that's why we've had to make revisions to the customer experience"

Matt Cooney
Chief Operating Officer
PA Housing

A Changing Sector

Technological advances are causing significant change, as the 'smart home' of inter-connected devices is getting ever closer. It is changing the housing sector, also. The observation near the start of the book that 'every business is a digital business these days' is a development that will only intensify.

Organisations will become more digital, with more similarities between them; there will be greater ease of transferability of skills between apparently different organisations as the marketing, communications and data security requirements between, say, a tourism agency, a social media company and a housing provider largely resemble one another. Notable among some of our interviewees for this book were professionals who had come to housing from another sector.

The need for social housing, at the time of writing, is as great as ever, and demand is still growing, with a growing population and house prices that remain relatively high, especially in the south of England. Political and demographic pressures are not going away, and will probably encourage much closer collaboration between housing and care providers.

Dan Moraga, Housing Project Manager at PA Housing, says: "There is pressure to build more. There is a big challenge to be efficient; that's probably why digital services will continue to be a big focus. Also, to build smarter homes, and make them smarter from the outset. We are starting to see people in private lives have lots of smart devices in their homes."

Kevin Hornsby, Head of Tenancy Sustainment at Orbit Housing, says: "There are a lot of challenges. One of the key ones is the lack of housing nationally. We are working to add 2,000 properties

> "There is still a housing shortage; there's a very clear drive to say we need more housing associations, and for them to become a more powerful group."

Julian Massel
Trafford Housing

a year. Waiting list demand is continuing to rise; temporary accommodation is continuing to be high."

He points also to the importance of welfare reform. Technology has been developing rapidly in the past 10 years, but it has done so at a time of austerity, in the wake of the banking crisis and curbs on public spending. The Government has imposed cuts on rents, with the aim of helping tenants, but putting pressure on the housing association business model. Universal Credit is a major reform. The aim is to simplify benefits and increase incentives to work. It puts more responsibility on individuals, and brings an element of risk, for housing associations and their tenants. "Universal Credit means customers have to manage their own money," says Kevin. "So the model we're looking at now is all about frontend, and dealing with customer need, and more advice and support at the start of the tenancy, which is quite different to how we've worked previously."

Julian Massel, Director of Technology at Trafford Housing, says there will be pressure for health and social care integration, parallel with the move towards more digitally connected houses and organisations: "There is still a housing shortage; there's a very clear drive to say we need more housing associations, and for them to become a more powerful group. There are a lot of merger

discussions. Housing of the future will [feature] smart cities, digital cities, there's a lot going on in that area."

Matt Cooney, Chief Operating Officer of PA Housing, says that four years of a 1% rent cut has taken a lot of money out of housing associations' business plans. "We felt that we were obliged to look at the operating model, and build digital in as a more reliable channel. That's the journey that inexorably we are on. If we can show that our operating costs are as efficient as can be, that helps us demonstrate value for money."

He has found that a strong opinion in government circles is that housing associations are inefficient, because they seek to generate a surplus from a subsidised activity. In some ways, it is an unfair view, as the surpluses are reinvested, but it is the political reality. "A reliable digital platform is obviously a way to demonstrate good value for money."

Political pressure, desire for efficiency and technological change could combine to make the housing provider of the future a rather different entity to the traditional housing association. It may well be working more closely with other service providers, as digital connectivity enhances the potential for collaboration, for example, between housing, social and health care providers, all with access to relevant data, subject to privacy protection and rights being maintained.

> **"A reliable digital platform is obviously a way to demonstrate good value for money."**
>
> **Matt Cooney**
> PA Housing

Conclusion

Key to the success and durability of the housing association has been its ability to innovate while maintaining the timeless principles of its founders – to create dignified living spaces for people on low incomes, including the most vulnerable. In the modern context, this means making the most of digital connectivity, both to improve efficiency in order to cope with austerity, and to improve and personalise services.

The sector has been slower to the digital *Shift* than other sectors such as banking and retail, but its leaders increasingly recognise this, and the pace at which it is catching up has accelerated in the past couple of years.

There is a need, almost a duty, to maintain this momentum, for the sake of the tenant.

Acknowledgements

First and foremost, we'd like to thank our interviewees for giving up their valuable time to speak to us and share their thoughts and experiences for this book.

Their insight has been invaluable and their willingness to support this project is a testament to the collaborative and open nature of the housing sector we've loved working within over the last 20 years.

Our interviewees:

Claire Bayliss, Director, 3C Consultants

Matt Cooney, Chief Operating Officer, Paragon Asra Housing

Steve Dungworth, Director of Digital Transformation, Accent

Rich Eden, Communications & Marketing Manager, Southway Housing Trust

Brian Halligan, CEO, Hubspot

Richard Harvey, Head of IT, Housing Solutions

Kevin Hornsby, Head of Tenancy Sustainment, Orbit

Julian Massell, Director of Transformation & Technology, Trafford Housing Trust

Robin Middleton, Head of Digital Marketing, Sovereign Housing Association

Daniel Moraga, Project Manager, Paragon Asra Housing

Paul Taylor, Innovation Lab Coach, Bromford

Boris Worrall, Chief Executive, Rooftop Housing Group

To all our current and past clients both inside and outside of the housing sector – thanks for your contribution too. We learn something new – no matter how small – through every project we do, and hopefully we've managed to pour that into this book.

Thanks to the 205 people who took part in our housing sector survey. In a sector that can be said to suffer from 'survey fatigue' from time to time, your patience and honesty in completing our survey is hugely appreciated.

We've drawn on the knowledge and experience of our own teams for this book too. The Prodo team always give their best to our clients and are passionate about building great working relationships that benefit everyone – including tenants. Their shared thoughts and experience have been invaluable in sense-checking, bolstering and expanding the scope of this book. Thanks to the whole team, but in particular to Ivo Kerkhof, Jacob Howell, Jenny Bradshaw, Paul Earnden and Sophie Everett, who've dedicated their time and energy to making this book what it is.

Last but not least, thanks to Philip Whiteley, for conducting the interviews and to Dan Reese and Craig Graham – thanks for your creative input in helping to bring the content of this book to life.